HOW TO
INFLUENCE
ANYONE
ANYWHERE
EVERY TIME

T0335207

Once upon a time...

On a humid, overcast day in March 1975, 24 school students sprawled at their desks awaiting the arrival of the new biology teacher. We hated biology. The previous teacher, who had left for personal reasons (fired), also hated the subject.

Then she arrived.

Miss Knight strode into the classroom with an energy and purpose that blew apart our complacent, wallowing disinterest.

She was carrying a battered leather briefcase. Old school. Belts and buckles. Second World War vibe. She chucked the thing onto a table, which landed with a meaty thud, before turning and glaring at all of us, smiling like Cruella and shouting, 'Right! Let's learn!'

I was 15 years old. The school was Thomas More College, near Durban in South Africa. I did not know it then, but this moment would change my life.

No surprise, biology became everyone's favourite subject. Miss Knight enthralled, challenged, provoked, engaged and immersed us in biological sciences with a relish and passion I can instantly recall decades later.

Influence

We communicate all the time. But do we influence?

COVID. Everyone is working from home. The chief financial officer (CFO) for a major division in one of the big Australian banks, let's call her Angela, found herself in front of her laptop, managing her team, doing CFO stuff on her dining room table. Her two daughters, both under 10, watched their mother working with interest.

After a few weeks, her nine-year-old asked, 'Mummy, what do you do for work?'

Angela explained, in nine-year-old terms, what managing finances entails before the nine-year-old said, '… but all you seem to do all day is talk. Do you talk for a living, Mummy? Or is your work just meetings?'

When Angela shared this experience with me, she commented, 'My daughter made me realise that mostly what I do all day is communicate. My job is to influence people to my way of thinking, and I'm not sure if I'm any good at it.'

This one question from her daughter changed how Angela approached her work.

Rather than being fixated on the accuracy of the data, I became more interested in the effectiveness of my communication. I had to learn how to communicate with emotion, energy and authority. One thing I learnt immediately was to look at the camera in virtual meetings. So simple. This alone changed the quality of connection with my team, my colleagues, my stakeholders.

Angela has driven this message home to her executive leadership team colleagues: 'Remember, we all *talk* for a living. Let's get better at this.'

Influence is critical in the business world.

Every professional, especially those in the corporate realm, is in the business of influence through communication. A simple shift in your perspective about the role and impact of your influence could revolutionise your professional journey, allowing you to leave an indelible mark and drive substantial change.

Angela delved deep into the essence of influence. This book does the same, offering practical insights, methodologies and examples to enhance your influence in your professional life, to reshape your organisation and drive change effectively.

This is a must-have tool for individuals and organisations aiming for success.

In business, having influence means having the power to affect others' decisions, actions and opinions.

It is as simple and as challenging as that.

How do we learn to communicate?

As a child you simply *absorbed* language and developed your early communication skills. If you were brought up in a multilingual environment, you learnt those languages too. How?

There is a delightful YouTube video of a young Italian girl, maybe four years old, in full flight talking about something or other.[1] Show anyone this video and ask them where she is from, the vast majority would say 'Italy' without hesitation. Her full gestural usage, that earnest facial expression and the tone of her voice all signal her roots. How did she learn to communicate like this?

It was another Italian, Giacoma Rizzolatti, who pioneered the research on the role mirror neurons play in how we learn.[2] Mirror neurons are a type of specialised brain cell, found in the premotor cortex and the inferior parietal cortex of the brain, to be specific. These neurons play a crucial role in understanding and *imitating* the actions and intentions of others.

The imitation mirror neurons enable is fundamental to language and communication development. When we see someone else speaking, using gestures and moving, mirror neurons fire in our brain, helping us mimic their actions. This imitation helps us learn the physical aspects of communication, such as how to form sounds, words and gestures.

Let's be clear, mirror neurons are not only responsible for language acquisition; they facilitate the learning process. When infants and young children observe and imitate the speech and gestures of their caregivers, mirror neurons play a role in helping them acquire language skills.

Why is this relevant? Because mirror neurons influence how you communicate at work.

Communication is a social process, and mirror neurons play a role in social learning. People imitate the behaviour of others for safety and to belong.

Cultural variances in the way people talk, move, dance, gesture, etc. are immediately recognisable. By observing and imitating the communication behaviours of others, we acquire language and adopt social norms, as well as all the cultural practices that will define your identity for the rest of your life.

Influence in the workplace

When you first started in the workplace, it was most likely a daunting experience to understand the cultural and professional expectations. Your mirror neurons were tracking everything: how people spoke, their tone, language, style, volume, gestures, postures — everything. Your brain was scanning for the rules of the game. 'How do I survive here?' It is an existential question being asked at a subconscious level.

We are going to challenge the norms and ways we currently communicate at work. Think of yourself as setting a new standard. You will influence the mirror neurons of your colleagues, your leaders, your customers and your friends simply by setting an example of superb communication skills.

This is even more important today where a lot of communication is done virtually. Effective and impactful communication is more necessary than ever.

Consider this:

- When you speak, do people lean in?

- After a meeting, do attendees leave with your face and your words locked into their minds?

- Once you have spoken or presented, do people feel impressed, challenged, provoked or inspired?

- How do you know?

dating to debating, from selling to seduction, from magnanimity to manipulation.

Professor Robert Cialdini's book *Influence, the Psychology of Persuasion*[4] shares six powerful principles of influence that are used to persuade individuals to comply with requests or adopt certain behaviours, attitudes or beliefs. We highly recommend Cialdini's work as it's practical and effective.

Our approach is to look at how to influence effectively at work using our methodology. We are often immersed in mundane, low-value, poor communication situations; for example, have you:

- been to a meeting that was a waste of time?

- had to endure a boring, irrelevant presentation?

- spoken up at a meeting and felt completely ignored?

- heard someone speak for a minute and had little or no understanding of what the hell they were talking about?

On the other hand:

- Have you felt out of place, lacking the confidence to say something for fear of being judged?

- Does the prospect of having to present something cause a storm of anxiety in your gut and mind?

- Have you said something in a meeting and then spent the rest of the meeting regretting it?

- Have you gone into a meeting unsure what it's about, and what role you are supposed to play, so you play neutral and safe?

- ◆ When you have to present to senior managers or leaders, do you feel super self-conscious and anxious about the impression you are making (or not)?

- ◆ Do you wish you could be as good a communicator as someone you know or work with?

What you are about to learn are the tools to turn you into a sophisticated, accomplished communicator, with the ability to influence anyone, anywhere, in every context, every time.

The skills you will learn, when practised and applied, will allow you to become a standout in how and what you communicate.

And it does take work.

You might be thinking: *I've never been comfortable with communicating in work environments. I always feel self-conscious and tongue-tied.* You are not alone, particularly when you are new to a job, early in your career and still learning the ropes. You will learn to let go of self-consciousness.

I don't mind meetings, but I hate presenting. As soon as I stand up, I feel stiff and awkward. This is something we hear frequently. Again, you will learn to look forward to opportunities to present.

It takes work though. These are not gimmicky techniques. This is skill development. The good news, though, is that we all communicate, all the time, every day. Every day is a practice day.

Let's start.

Thank you, Bernice McCarthy

A Canadian school teacher, Bernice McCarthy, published a book in 1980, on her research and application of a framework she called 4-Mat.[5]

It's elegance itself, and we would encourage you to read more about her work. We have applied her framework for the classroom to corporate communication. Figure 1 breaks it down.

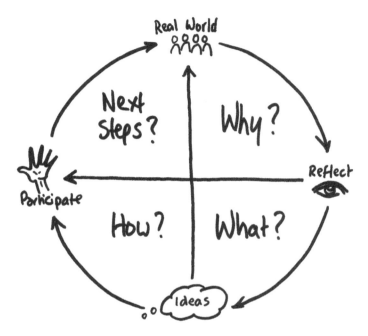

Figure 1: Bernice McCarthy's 4-Mat Model

Phase 1: The Why? Frame: The model starts with the people you are communicating with, be that a presentation audience, participants in a meeting or workshop, or a one-on-one conversation.

What is their 'real world' like? What are their concerns, challenges, issues, motivations, hopes and aspirations?

You can delve into this by starting with their backgrounds. LinkedIn and online searches usually provide a ton of stuff on people's background, career pathways, interests, associations and the like. In a work context, you may know some of this already, but diving a bit deeper also allows you to understand the person beyond the work persona.

For example, by doing a 'real-world' diagnosis of a chief revenue officer, we learnt from his LinkedIn profile that he had played professional football (the American version), could speak four languages and was a volunteer at a homeless shelter in New York City. From this, we could reasonably conclude that he had the discipline of a professional sportsperson, had a worldview wider than his own country and cared about social justice. We also noticed that he tended to change roles every two years, ascending the corporate ladder at speed. We guessed he was super competent, impressive in manner and decisive in how he managed himself and others. This was confirmed when we met him.

In our diagnose phase we ask questions like: What do you see as the biggest challenges currently facing your industry, and how is your company adapting to these challenges? This question helps us understand the external factors affecting the industry and the executive's strategic response.

The more data and insight you can get on the individuals and the context they work in, the clearer you will be in appreciating and understanding their everyday reality.

From there we can design a compelling *Why? Frame* (relevance). The audience will see that the communication is relevant, meaningful and worthwhile, and will likely engage and move to be active participants in the conversation, meeting or presentation.

The *Why? Frame* is critical. We will go into much more detail in Chapter 3 when we explore the design and content of a compelling relevance story. Remember, you will only be interested in something if you have a reason, a 'why', to explore it further.

Phase 2: The What? Frame: The Why? Frame leads to the content or ideas you want to share, which we call the *What? Frame*.

Phase 3: The How? Frame: Once your audience understands the What, you can move to explore the implications and applications, which is the *How? Frame*. This turns your ideas into action.

Phase 4: The Next Steps? Frame: Finally, what happens next?

Have you ever left a meeting not knowing if you are supposed to do anything? Worse, have you left wondering what the purpose of the meeting was in the first place? This suggests that there was no agreement on next steps.

An effective *Next Steps? Frame* means everyone is crystal clear on personal and collective accountabilities and responsibilities. Again, we will plunge deeper into this in Part II when we look at design work.

Foundation: It's all about the Triple D

Eight years ago while Erica was designing a Masterclass on Pitching, she was drawing on her 30 years of sales experience to unpack the core method she used in her customer conversations. As she unpacked it, she realised the three core elements of Diagnose, Design and Deliver that she applied naturally in her sales process were true of all quality engagements and communication. The Triple D model has become the underpinning for all of the elements in our communication methodology The Colin James Method.

As you explore the following chapters and your own experience, you'll realise we need to include these steps in every communication context at work and in life. Miss one of the steps and you'll find people leave a meeting or conversation without full understanding and as a consequence re-work, multiple meetings, misunderstandings and all sorts of unproductive outcomes will be the result.

You are sitting in a meeting. You have something to say regarding the current conversation happening around the table or Zooming over the internet.

- ◆ Step 1: You assess what is being discussed and decide to add to the mix.

♦ Step 2: You think about what you'll say, not necessarily thoroughly, but you have an idea.

♦ Step 3: You find the chance to intervene and say your piece.

That's it.

To put it simply, you *diagnosed* the situation, *designed* a response in your head, and then spoke, or *delivered* your words

This is the Triple D process:

1. Diagnose

2. Design

3. Delivery

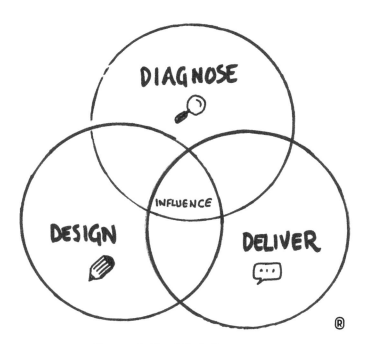

Figure 2: The Triple D process
*The Diagnose Design Deliver model is a registered trademark
of Altmore International Pty Ltd*

While this looks so simple — it's just three words — each step requires deep work, disciplined structure and thoughtful consideration. In all our work, we bang the Triple D drum constantly. If your communication fails to achieve its outcome, you will find that you most likely miscalculated or missed key elements in one or more of the Triple D elements.

Influence will occur if you *diagnose* the context intelligently; *design* a response in a clear way; and then *deliver* with the right tone and technique to ensure you are heard and understood (see figure 2).

Diagnose

'I think you saved my career.' I was on a Zoom call with an executive general manager for one of the major banks in November 2022.

> *I applied what I had learnt about diagnosing your audience before my presentation to the executive leadership team and the board. What I learnt on your program about preparation and stakeholder management allowed me to rethink my whole approach. If I hadn't followed your structure, I would be in a world of pain right now.*

In our experience, way too many people sabotage themselves through poor diagnoses of the context, the people and a lack of focus on the outcome in communication settings.

It's like someone arriving at a hospital emergency room without triage. It's just a superficial guess at what the patient might need. Sadly, this is the norm in corporate communication, but our method demands more rigour and prep before any communication event.

In the following chapters, we will deep dive into how to effectively diagnose a situation and determine what the audience's real world consists of.

Design

We were having a debrief meeting with a global technology leader after he delivered his keynote in Dubai. He has been an advocate of the Colin James Method for over 20 years.

> *What always astounds me is how your design methodology works. Seeing 500 delegates shift from sceptical to neutral to intrigued to convinced in 20 minutes is beautiful to behold. We must build true believers in the CJM 'nail the opening' methodology.*

A home builder follows an architectural plan. The design of the house starts on the page. Excellent communication requires the same discipline. Too many times I've heard people say 'I'll just wing it', before delivering a low-quality, time-wasting presentation. Poor design leads to poor delivery.

Delivery

On a leadership offsite at a major insurance company in Brisbane, Australia, a speaker was invited onto the stage before lunch to share some views of the current quality of service being delivered through the company's call centres.

The morning sessions had been filled with the usual PowerPoint presentations, and the 50 or so people in the room were already jaded and numbed by the deluge of data that had been dumped during the day.

Maria walked onto the stage in a quiet and unassuming manner. No lectern. No slides. Just her in the middle of the stage.

Twelve minutes later, she thanked the audience and walked off. There was a weird silence as she descended the stairs before a clamour of applause filled the room, and everyone burst into loud conversations with colleagues about the insights they had heard from Maria.

Maria started with a story of tears. How, at the end of each shift, some of her call centre colleagues weep at the frustration and stress they face every day from customers, who are often at a very difficult time in their lives, and who find the experience of endless waiting on phones for people who cannot help them because of the confusion and complexity of the company's policies an awful and degrading experience. And the punching bags are the call centre operators.

Maria spoke with quiet authority. Her tone was balanced but shot through with steel and purpose. Her demand of the leadership team was simple: get your act together fast.

No PowerPoint slides, no notes, no carefully scripted corporate language. She spoke plainly. Her posture was strong. Her voice was convincing. No one doubted that this 23-year-old had every right to stand on the stage. Her impact was profound. She changed how call centre management, resourcing and support were done in her organisation. In 12 minutes.

You will learn the same.

PART I
DIAGNOSE

I realised how often I go into meetings and presentations without a clear idea of who is in the room. I'm embarrassed to say that I have gone into high-stakes meetings knowing little or nothing about the people I'm supposedly going to influence. My excuse was always time. I now see how essential the diagnose phase is, and the results have been spectacular.

Email from a regional vice president, technology sector, Florida, USA

Using the triage analogy, a diagnosis implies a thorough analysis and understanding of the communication context you are preparing for, be it a conversation, a meeting or a presentation.

Influencing people starts with understanding who is in the room, the context, the outcome, and creating a compelling reason why they should listen to you.

Time to work

Think of an important or high-stakes conversation, meeting or presentation you have coming up. If there isn't one in the near future, think of a situation you are likely to face. The following chapters will guide you through the stages of diagnose, design and deliver step-by-step. Be prepared to brainstorm some ideas at each stage of the process. We will prompt you with ideas and questions to get your creativity flowing.

CHAPTER 1

DIAGNOSING THE WHAT AND THE WHO

Diagnosis starts because there is an event, an important meeting or a key presentation in your calendar. It could be an important conversation or even an interview. Capturing the relevant information for the context is the first step.

What is the context?

What you call the communication 'event' matters (see figure 1.1, overleaf). A meeting is different from a discussion. A discussion is different from a debate. If it is in your control, frame the context to serve the audience and outcome. Take these examples:

> *'Hi Julie, is it possible to have a quick* chat *about the project for about 30 minutes?'*

'Julie, we need to have a meeting *about the project; 30 minutes should cover it.'*

'Can we workshop *an idea for the project, Julie? Thirty minutes max?'*

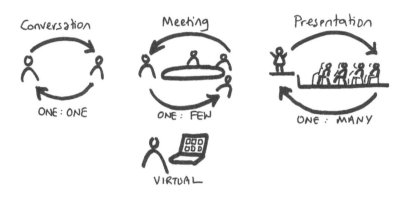

Figure 1.1: Communication contexts

Each of these scenarios is 30 minutes; however, the name provides a different context from Julie's point of view.

Obviously, in a one-to-many situation, it could be a presentation, pitch, workshop or panel discussion. Once you've defined the context, the next step is to describe your role. This is straightforward if you are leading the meeting or are the keynote speaker. Often, though, you are part of a team where you could be adding your expertise for a section of the conversation or presentation. This influences the later design and delivery elements.

Finally, the next step is to identify whether it is an in-person event versus a pure virtual or blended set-up. Again, this will inform the next step: your design (see Part II).

Time to work

Think back to the high-stakes conversation, meeting or presentation you identified on page 2. Describe the context and your role using these prompting questions.

- What is the type of communication? Is it a presentation, meeting, pitch, briefing, workshop or conversation?

- What is your role? Are you the leader, a contributor or participant?

- Is the event virtual or live?

What is the topic, subject or theme?

I had a conversation with an executive who is taking his leadership team to an offsite.

'What is the purpose of the two days?' I asked.

'We will do some strategy work, team building, that sort of thing ... '

Of course, I challenged him.

'You are taking 12 people away, for two nights and two-and-a-half days to a lovely rural property, and the theme of this leadership offsite is "strategy, team building, that sort of thing"?'

Being explicit about the topic, subject or theme of the communication event is critical for your following design work in Part II. Specificity is the key to this.

At this stage, you describe the big picture, the conceptual frame, for the communication session. Often this is very straightforward; for example, this could be an annual performance review. Done.

We have worked with clients on their annual sales kick-off meetings, and when asked what the core theme is, we hear the same old generic descriptions: 'one team', 'succeeding together', 'winning mindset'.

These themes are common and generic, and this dilutes their intended impact. Over the past ten years or so, we have been part of 12 different conferences and events where the theme was 'Evolve'. The organisers thought their event theme was unique and clearly captured the sentiment. Evolve is a fine word. As a theme, it's bland and, to use a wonderfully descriptive word, a bit meh.

Some years ago, I was speaking at an event at Manly, Sydney. The theme was 'There be dragons'.

What do you think of when reading those words: 'There be dragons'? Curiosity? Intrigue? Confusion? Interest?

These are all better emotive responses than 'meh'.

The master of ceremonies walked on and opened with 'There be dragons' in a classic pirate voice. He went on to explain that 'there be dragons' is a phrase that has its roots in medieval mapmaking. During the Middle Ages, cartographers would often include illustrations of dragons, sea serpents and other mythological creatures on uncharted areas of maps. These depictions served as symbols for unknown territories and dangers, essentially warning explorers of the potential perils they might face in these unexplored regions. The theme related to the unchartered waters the company strategy was heading towards. Clever theme. Memorable. Better than 'Evolve'.

This also applies to presentation titles. If you were attending a presentation on 'Risk management and mitigation', you may assume it's going to be something super technical and potentially dull. Calling the presentation 'Risky business: Mastering the art of safe play' would get more attention. It's more likely to build intrigue.

Time to work

Building on from the previous exercise where you identified your context, describe the central theme of your communication.

For example, is it a project update, delivering research results, discussing strategy, planning for Q4, brainstorming the risk challenges of artificial intelligence, tracking marketing performance, sharing leadership challenges, and so on? Be specific. Name the project. For example. 'Four-week progress report on Project Delphi', 'Employee survey results November/December', 'Reworking the GTM to counter Microsoft' — or be creative and find your own 'dragons' title.

Who is who?

A question we often ask at the start of our programs is: 'How many of you find people fascinating?' followed by 'How many of you find yourselves fascinating?'

Human beings are complex systems. We are all trying to utilise a blend of our physiological, psychological, neurological, emotional and intellectual systems at any given moment. We are riddled with programmed biases; operating on a myriad of foundational beliefs and value systems; dealing with the simple challenges of living our own lives; not to mention the complexities of families, relationships, collegial stuff, personal ambitions and various proclivities from the mundane to the weird.

It's almost arrogant to think we have the ability to influence anyone given the knotted complexity any human being is at any given moment.

The more you understand the psychological, intellectual and emotional make-up of another person, the more likely you will be able to communicate with greater accuracy and relevance. We are all guilty of being too superficial in our understanding and appreciation of others.

Not too many years ago, I worked with a business leader in the banking sector. This was one-on-one coaching, helping him establish his leadership brand. His ambition was to ascend to the executive leadership table, and ultimately be a CEO of a large financial sector organisation. At our first meeting, I asked him to give me a little insight into his background. I had his professional history, of course.

I had made some assumptions. In my mind, he had been born into a fairly wealthy, connected family, had attended good schools where he excelled, and achieved similar results at university. The story I made up in my mind was that he was fast-tracked because of his intellectual clout and the power of his network — perhaps with some family influences thrown into the mix.

Wrong.

He came from an extremely modest (and brutal) background. He was the antithesis of privilege. One of his driving values was supporting struggling people in our communities. Knowing this allowed us to tailor our work precisely. My original assumption could have left me focusing on purely commercial outcomes, driving up the share price and running a lean, clean operational machine. Instead, I realised his purpose was deeper than standard business objectives. We focused on building his leadership philosophy, his messaging and how he could contribute to customer and community benefit while still meeting or exceeding commercial goals.

Influencing starts with understanding, appreciating and respecting the people who you will be communicating with, and we need to start with the basics.

So how do you diagnose who's who in the room?

There are numerous ways you can diagnose who is going to be receiving your communication. Some scenarios (such as a weekly meeting) will obviously be easier than others (such as delivering a keynote speech to a conference).

Time to work

Let's get specific. Now that you know your context, identify the key stakeholders. What are their names, roles and locations? Are they supporters, resistors, sponsors, neutral or hostile? Ask around, use experience, use others' experience, stay awake to how people you work with operate. Look for patterns. To be a person of influence, you have to be profoundly interested in the people you are seeking to influence and support.

LINKEDIN

Depending on the size of the audience, you could choose to access the LinkedIn profiles of everyone in the room. You may have access to other platforms, both internal and external, where biographical information can be sourced. Researching this gives you foundational information, from which you can look for patterns, anomalies, points of interest and the like.

We sometimes get pushback from people suggesting this is too time consuming. The decision you have to make is how effective do you want to be as a communicator, as a person of influence? We don't question exceptional athletes for working harder, longer and with more discipline than their fellow athletes, so why would it be any different for exceptional influencers?

To give you some perspective, one graduate program we run has over 200 delegates, and I, personally, spend eight hours researching each and every participant, demonstrating to them, in the early days of their career journey, that preparation is the breakfast of champions.

Analysing someone's LinkedIn profile can provide a wealth of information about their professional background, skills and network. Here are some key aspects to focus on:

PROFILE SUMMARY AND HEADLINE

The summary and headline give an immediate impression of the person's professional identity. Look for keywords that point to their industry, expertise and professional interests. Some summaries are chatty and personable, providing a sense of personality and style.

EXPERIENCE SECTION

This is crucial for understanding their career path. Look at their job titles, the companies they've worked for, the duration of each role, and the responsibilities and achievements listed. This tells you not only about their experience, but also about their career progression and stability.

EDUCATION

Check their educational background to understand their foundational knowledge and skills. This includes not just degrees, but also certifications and special courses.

SKILLS AND ENDORSEMENTS

This section shows what skills they consider important and how many people have endorsed them for these skills. It's a good indicator of their strengths as perceived by their peers.

RECOMMENDATIONS

Written recommendations provide insights into how colleagues and superiors view the individual. They can reveal aspects of their work ethic, team dynamics and professional impact.

ACTIVITY

Reviewing their posts, comments and shares can give you a sense of their professional interests, views and how they engage with their network.

ACCOMPLISHMENTS

Look for any awards, publications, projects, patents or speaking engagements. These can highlight special achievements and areas of expertise.

VOLUNTEER EXPERIENCE

This can provide insight into their personal interests and values, as well as additional skills.

CONNECTIONS AND NETWORK

The size and nature of their network can be telling. Look at who they are connected with — peers, industry leaders, diverse professions, etc.

GROUPS AND ASSOCIATIONS

Membership of professional groups suggests areas of interest and ongoing engagement in professional development.

***

Remember, the LinkedIn profile presents a carefully curated version of a person's professional self — it won't tell you the *whole* story.

REPUTATION

The assessment of whether a participant is a sponsor, supporter, neutral, resistor or hostile can be drawn from your own experience in most scenarios; however, getting perspectives from a wider group of people increases the accuracy of the diagnosis.

In preparing a client for a major career move, we did the diagnosis on the people on the interview committee. There was one HR person who was an unknown quantity. Reputation research identified that the HR person was famous for being belligerent and challenging. Further digging revealed that this HR exec did the belligerent routine as a test of resilience to assess how the interviewee managed threat and stress. To discover this, we connected with people in his network, read their LinkedIn articles and posts, and found a few articles in trade journals. One article in an HR magazine covered his 'good cop, bad cop' routine in how he conducts interviews. It was all there.

'If I hadn't done the diagnostic, I would have found it extremely difficult not to take it personally. He went into full a-hole mode', our client told us later.

He got the job.

Big audiences

All hands, town halls, conferences, events and the like are a one-to-many delivery. Here the diagnosis is to find out what the current sentiments, concerns and issues are in play. Where we have seen poor diagnosis time and time again is in internal all hands presentations. This also becomes more challenging in virtual contexts.

One client in the banking industry in England was disturbed to discover that about 50 per cent of their staff logged onto an all hands call remotely rather than attending in person. Because of tech issues, they stopped the all hands after 12 minutes, letting everyone know that the meeting would be held two days later. Only half of the attendees logged off; the other half were not at their desks to hear the news of the cancellation. Their managers were notified to follow up. Many excuses were made ... everyone knew the truth. The employees logged in to demonstrate attendance and then did other stuff.

The feedback to the organisers was clear. The all hands calls were so bad, so irrelevant, that 50 per cent of their employees found other things to do, perhaps catching up with the latest episode of *Love Island*. Who knows?

Big audiences require a much more considered relevance design. Attend any live conference and stand at the back of the room. People vote with their devices. If the speaker is seen as irrelevant to them, their heads drop to their phones or similar.

CHAPTER 2

WHAT IS THE OUTCOME FROM THE AUDIENCE PERSPECTIVE?

This one question, 'What is the outcome from the *audience* perspective?', changes the focus and attention and immediately puts you into a position of influence (see figure 2.1, overleaf). The reason is the vast majority of people enter communication contexts with the outcome *they* want first and foremost.

We were working with a client planning a conference, and the theme was 'Stronger Together'. Not an uncommon sentiment. In discussion with the executive sponsor, he led with:

> *I want to ensure greater unity and commitment to the strategy. I want them to appreciate the opportunity we have and also the challenges we are facing. I also want them to have some fun, so it's not just a session full of PowerPoint slides.*

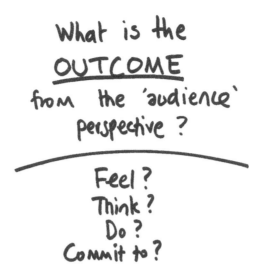

Figure 2.1: Focusing on the outcome

This *I want* approach was the first mistake in the diagnostic.

The word 'audience' refers to anyone who will be part of the communication event. Replace the word 'audience' with colleague, stakeholder, customer, team, manager, executive leader, partner, supplier or friend. The key focus is seeing things from their perspective: their needs, their wants, their concerns and their reality. What will they feel, think, do and commit to?

As soon as your audience senses that your intention is for *their* benefit, the quality of their attention immediately lifts.

What do you want them to feel?

Influence occurs when trust is the currency. Are you more likely to believe a close friend or colleague or a stranger? Do you believe the salesperson or a review by a customer who has used the product or service? Belief leads to trust. Once trust is earned, your ability to influence is elevated exponentially.

Humans are fundamentally creatures of emotion, despite our claims of rationality and logic. Our decisions are hugely influenced by our feelings.

Think about it, based purely on the data, no one would get married. Statistically you have a 50 per cent chance of failure given about 50 per cent of marriages end in divorce in most Western cultures.

We don't make decisions through logic alone — emotions are fundamental to being convinced by anything. You cannot measure love. You cannot quantify the joy of family.

Influence starts with emotion.

In your diagnosis, you may be working with people who are anxious and uncertain about recent changes or restructures. If you don't acknowledge this, or respect it, your positive message could be lost or discounted.

Your assessment of the current emotional state of your audience is fundamental to you creating the conditions for successful influence. If the destination is for your audience to leave with positive feelings, such as inspired, excited and motivated, you need to determine their current state before you can design your communication to achieve the desired state or outcome.

Your audience could be curious, disengaged, anxious, compliant (showing up because they have to), negative or bored. If you misread or misdiagnose the *current* state, you will find it extremely difficult to get your audience to the *desired* state.

Now the focus moves to the emotional outcome. At the end of your communication, have you influenced your audience (and remember, this can be an audience of one) to feel inspired, confident, relieved, challenged, engaged, excited or calm?

This 'feeling' outcome will inform your messages, your framing and, most importantly, your stories.

What do you want them to think?

Have you ever attended a presentation where you felt patronised or talked down to by the presenter?

We have all sat in meetings where stuff is being presented or discussed that has little or no relevance to us, or maybe to anything at all. We've all heard someone share a thought that simply drifted past like a dandelion seed on a balmy afternoon breeze.

To engage someone intellectually, where what you share or say focuses their attention, is at the heart (and mind) of effective influence.

As we have discussed, people are complex, and when people are actively listening, they are running a number of neurological programs. This includes assessment for truth or veracity; logical reasoning; comparison to existing information; references to past experiences; imagination (of possible futures); and judgement on top of the standard set of filters of values, beliefs, self-interest, ego, id and super-ego dynamics.

We were working with a newly hired business leader who was deciding on the make-up of his leadership team. In our discussions, he praised his head of operations for her diligence and extraordinary grasp of the detail in a complicated manufacturing business. Three months later, I checked in with his progress and asked about his leadership team. 'Well, I got rid of the head of ops and found someone much more suitable.' Bewildered, I asked him to explain how someone he was so impressed with could lose favour so quickly. 'Oh, I found out that she had no tertiary qualifications. Can you believe it? I'm not sure how she got this far in her career.'

This is cognitive bias (where we favour one perception or idea over another, often without evidence). And we all have them. Part of your ability to influence is knowing how to frame content or your message to get past prejudices, limiting beliefs and even hostility.

We are seeing fundamentalism becoming more entrenched, meaning that facts and data are invalidated by someone's beliefs, regardless of their merit. This is why we start with managing the emotional stuff (feelings) first.

To challenge someone's intellectual architecture and enhance or develop their thinking requires careful management of information in a way that people can comprehend. How many times have you been inundated with copious amounts of data where the presenter says '... now you won't be able to read this' as they display a dense slide filled with stuff that would take five minutes to read, let alone understand.

Content is not communicating. Content alone does not influence. Content is the refuge of the insecure.

Shifting someone's thinking is a combination of framing and input: creating the optimal neurological conditions for someone to allow information to direct their attention and behaviour.

What do you want them to do?

While we call this the 'call to action' element, it's more sophisticated than it appears on the surface. The ultimate test of influence is behavioural change.

I may *feel* that being healthy and fit will enhance the quality of my life and enhance my happiness.

I may *know* (think) what diet to follow and what exercise regime to follow.

But if I don't *do* anything, I have not been influenced. I have meaning and knowledge, but there is no change.

Not all communication results in behavioural change. Staying informed, understanding what's going on, and being aware of the important stuff is, of course, important.

Your ability to influence will be elevated by connecting content (understanding) to action, making your message more impactful. Think of this as looking at implication (what does this mean?) and application (how do you use this?).

What do you want them to commit to?

One question to ask yourself about meetings is: 'What are the likely consequences if this next meeting is cancelled?' Let's be honest, the consequence would often be negligible or, worse, neither negative nor positive.

Accountability drives behaviour change. Focusing on what happens after your conversation, meeting or presentation increases the likelihood of influence. Next, we are going to explore simple statements that drive commitment and accountability.

Time to work

At the end of your presentation, what will the audience:

- Feel: Will they be excited, inspired, relieved, challenged, concerned, pumped, trusting, convinced, etc?

- Think: What new knowledge, insight, data, information or perspective will they now have?

- Do: What will they pilot, stop, start, agree to, engage with, fund, continue?

- Commit to: How will they tangibly demonstrate commitment? What are the check-in points and measurability?

CHAPTER 3
BEGIN WITH WHY

Start With Why is a best-selling book by Simon Sinek.[6] He states that the simplest idea is to answer the question 'What's in it for me?' that every person asks in almost any communication context.

The reality is that relevance, or the Why? Frame, is often ignored, assumed or superficially handled.

> *Every Tuesday morning, we have to attend the weekly sales meeting. We have to present our sales, pipeline and forecast, and there are 16 of us. It takes 90 minutes. The only thing anyone is interested in is ensuring they don't make a mistake in their numbers. A total waste of time.*

We have heard variations of this many, many times. It only takes a few minutes to define the relevance and purpose of a meeting. However, if relevance is ignored or the why? is assumed, the level of engagement plummets.

Two primary forces drive human motivation (see figure 3.1, overleaf):

1. move away

2. move towards.

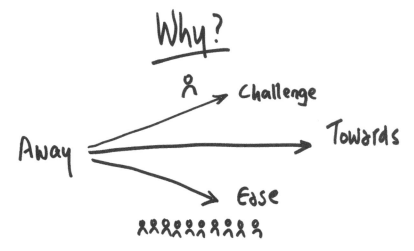

Figure 3.1: People are motivated away and towards

We are motivated away from things we don't want: loss, shame, pain, poverty, failure, loneliness and so on. Or we are motivated towards things we do want: gain, pride, pleasure, wealth, success, love, etc.

Of course, complex human beings are influenced by biological, psychological, cognitive, economic, cultural and social drivers. And we can plunge deep into each of these, however, the foundations will stem from our push/pull drives. We don't have the carrot-and-stick analogy for nothing.

Time to work

Reflect on the following questions.

Start with you: Why do you care? What's in it for you? Do you believe in your topic/content? Do you care? If you don't care, how can you find purpose and relevance for you personally?

Now, think about your audience: Sit in their seat: Why would they be interested in your communication? What reason do they have to pay attention?

Next, focus on the pain points: What is the *personal* cost or risk to the audience of not knowing, learning, or applying what they are about to hear?

What do they have to gain: What is the *personal* benefit or advantage of knowing, learning or applying what they are about to hear and learn?

Finally, what is the collective relevance: What are the benefits to the organisation/business, the customer, the community, etc.?

Map the territory

We now know the three steps in the diagnose phase:

1. *Who* comprises the audience for the conversation, meeting, presentation or event?

2. What is the *outcome* from the audience's perspective?

3. How can you build a compelling *relevance* case?

The final stage is to map your content. Not script. Map.

It's amazing how our lives are defined by specific moments in time. In 1995, I was sitting in a room of fellow learners on a life-changing program facilitated by Marvin Oka. Marvin hails from Hawaii and is an extraordinary man who gave me the foundations for my career as an educator.

On this day, Marvin introduced a framework for managing content. This model changed my life and still serves me every day. It looks so simple, but there is disguised complexity, as you will discover. What it does is build a logic tree in organising information or content. Marvin called it the CPD (concept, principles, details) Hierarchy (see figure 3.2).

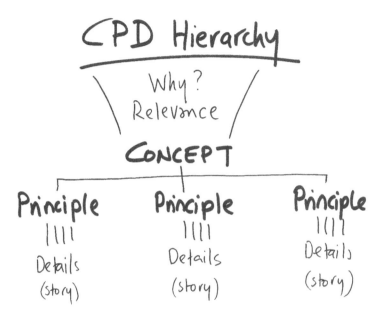

Figure 3.2: The concept, principles, details (CPD) hierarchy

A simple example of a CPD Hierarchy is the structure of the book, *The 7 Habits of Highly Effective People* by Stephen Covey.[7]

The *concept* tells you exactly what you will learn.

The *principles* are each of the habits: a chapter for each habit.

The *details* explain each habit, with examples and stories to validate and illustrate.

CPD Hierarchy has one incredibly powerful effect on your audience or meeting participants: it reduces the cognitive load. The human working memory has limited capacity, and it can only hold a small amount of information at once. Structuring your content into CPD groups related pieces of information together into larger, meaningful chunks. This reduces the cognitive load and makes it easier to process and remember information. It's as simple as that.

CPD Hierarchy encourages you to apply the principle of chunking: organising your content into neurologically friendly, bite-sized chunks.

Around the same time, Barbara Minto developed a similar model called the Minto Pyramid Model,[8] which is used widely in the consulting industry. Her framework was developed during her time at McKinsey & Company over 40 years ago, and is worth a Google.

Chunking

Chunking is a concept in cognitive psychology that refers to organising and grouping information into smaller, more manageable units or 'chunks'. This is why the CPD Hierarchy is so powerful. It helps people process and remember information more effectively by reducing the cognitive load on working memory.

If I asked you to remember five random objects, let's say:

1. door

2. seagull

3. towel

4. wine bottle

5. rose

you would most likely remember them.

If I asked you to remember 20 random objects, you would struggle. If I said, please remember these 45 objects, that would be impossible.

However, if I said, 'Remember these 20 items, five relate to a house, five to a garden, five to shed and five to birds', your chances of recalling all 20 would improve dramatically. This is the power of CPD and chunking. We will expand on how this applies to visual aids in Chapter 16.

Time to work

Think of a concept you are planning to communicate to a group, in a meeting or at a plenary. Use the CPD Hierarchy to break down the ideas into manageable chunks.

Think about your content design by writing down the 'what' and the 'how' in more detail. Try and catch your audience's attention by encapsulating the idea in a short, snappy headline.

From your headline, pull out three principles that give your audience the broad idea of the concept. This is the what, not the how.

Each of the three principles needs more detail so your audience knows what to do next or what will happen next. Think about the story, example, process, activity and how that applies to your message and the outcome you are leading towards.

The following is an example of a CPD template, used by an executive, delivering at an investment event in Singapore a few years ago. This was the end product of a lot of deep diagnosis and deep design.

Using your situation as the case study, begin building your own CPD structure using this template.

Concept (headline):	Success in the education industry
	Punchy, memorable, six words or fewer

Principle One	Principle Two	Principle Three
Current challenges	Many solutions	The market awaits

Principle One details: *Story/data/example/process/analogy/activity*
Huge demand, Education expensive relative to GDP, Affordability, Harvard example, Poverty alleviation

Principle Two details: *Story/data/example/process/analogy/activity*
Incremental change, Bottom up, Market adaptability, Sukram Story

Principle Three details: *Story/data/example/process/analogy/activity*
Australia: Post COVID opportunity, Africa: Micro credentialling, degrees, Europe: England not only choice, USA: Active recruitment

'Give me the CPD first, then I will read the report.' This is the direction a regional VP of an AI technology company gives his team. 'When I first learnt CPD from you, I applied the framework to all my spoken and written comms. It has been a tool I've used daily.'

Complete your CPD map *before* you think about slides or visual aids.

Now that you have completed the diagnose phase, you know the following:

◆ who your audience is in detail

◆ the outcome they will experience using feel, think, do and commit to as a guide

◆ the relevant messages and approach that will work for them

◆ a content map structured using the CPD framework.

This is deep work. Having a deep insight into the current state of your audience allows you to manage the conversation and messaging to support the attainment of the desired state. To do this, and do this well, we must now move to *design*.

PART II
DESIGN

From an interview with a middle manager in the fast-moving consumer goods industry.

I'm embarrassed to acknowledge this, but in the past, my so-called design was a slide deck with speaker notes linked to each slide. I would click through the slides and read the notes aloud. In my defence, I thought this was how it was supposed to be done. What I now realise is that effective design is done way before we even consider slides or visual aids. I now find I hardly ever use slides because my design is so on point, so clear, so compelling that the slides become a hindrance rather than of value.

The world's greatest theatre experiences start with words on a page. Multibillion-dollar blockbuster movies start with a script, a design, of the narrative and scenes. Iconic fashion is drawn first, by hand, onto sheets of paper.

Communication is no different. Design is fundamental to success. We are not simply dumping data, we are bringing meaning, value and illumination into the heads, hearts and gut of everyone who is listening to us in any and every communication context. Let's learn how.

The 12 steps (no alcohol involved)

In every communication situation, we follow a structure. Most of the time this is not consciously done; it's more or less copied from those who have gone before us.

We were talking to young banking graduates after one of our programs when one of them, Xiang, asked 'Why are meetings run the way they are? Is there a best practice approach? I personally find meetings to be ineffectual, poor use of my time and generally frustrating.'

Her question points to the reality that the 'how we do things around here' attitude becomes normalised with too little analysis on effectiveness or value.

There are many, many books providing guidance on better ways to communicate in specific contexts, such as how to give feedback (*Fixing Feedback* by Georgia Murch[9] is a standout), how to conduct an interview, package a presentation, run a meeting … the list goes on.

What we outline below are the 12 steps essential to any communication context. They include:

1. Start *strong* (grab the attention/interest of the audience)

2. Create *relevance* (why will this audience/customer need/want to know this?)

3. Introduce your *concept* (topic)

4. Manage the FODs (fears, objections and doubts)

5. Self-intro (earning the right and creating a personal connection)

6. Guidelines (what behaviour do you want from the audience?)

7. Reintroduce the *concept*

8. Lay out your *principles* (use anchoring)

9. Present *details* (core content/stories)

10. Summarise by re-emphasising the *principles* (use the same anchoring points)

11. Call to action: the ask/next steps (use the anchoring timeline)

12. Close (loop back to the start strong and relevance and confirm next steps).

While this might seem cumbersome (and long), the steps are not time dependent. Like any model, there is scope to leave some steps out; for example, Step 5 might be redundant with people who know you well. However, there is also value in using Step 5 to deepen your credibility in some situations.

We will be going into each step in detail. You will use your diagnose work to help flesh out the fields in your design.

The five phases

In our research, we have identified five phases that, when followed, produce excellent communication outcomes.

◆ Phase one: Establishing *context* creates meaning, relevance and purpose.

◆ Phase two: Building *connection* establishes credibility and relationships.

- Phase three: Exploring *content* delivers information, data, ideas and stories.

- Phase four: A *call to action* delivers implications and applications.

- Phase five: *Close* wraps it up and set up the next steps.

Phase one: Context

Think about a recent presentation you observed. Did it follow this flow?

Slide: *bearing the presenter's name and the presentation topic's name*.

The presenter walks on and starts with: 'Good morning, thank you for being here today, I appreciate how busy you are. My name is Clifford Glover, and I'm the head of marketing. What I'm going to talk to you about today is our new go-to-market strategy.'

Slide: *Showing a detailed agenda*

'Let me start with the agenda' (reads agenda).

Slide: *Complex slide of boxes, arrows and small text*

'Now you probably won't be able to read this, apologies for that, however, what you are looking at is the detailed outline of our GTM model from market analysis, segmentation, product mix, persona and sales assets ...'

Sound familiar? This is pretty standard structure ...

- Greeting

- Self-intro

- Topic

- Content

What is missing in the flow is the first of the 5 Cs: context.

You've have heard the phrase 'all meaning is contextual'. If a man is walking down a city street and is suddenly attacked by two men, crushing him to the ground, we would call that an assault. If it occurs on a rugby field and the man is carrying a ball, we would applaud the tacklers. Same behaviour, different context, different meaning. A medical HR executive told us:

> *We realised that many of our regular meetings were context-free. They were called things like ops meetings and other vague titles, but the value of bringing people together to share stuff and updates was not apparent. We are now adamant that meetings have an explicit purpose. Context is critical.*

The key to setting the context is creating curiosity, interest and relevance for your audience. We use the first four steps of the 12-step model to establish a clean, relevant context.

1. Start strong (grab the attention/interest of the audience)

2. Create relevance (why will this audience/customer need/want to know this?)

3. Introduce your concept (topic)

4. Manage the FODs (fears, objections and doubts)

Phase two: Connection

Most people will introduce themselves straight away unless they're already well known to each other. It's a straightforward act of courtesy.

Our research reveals that the *connection* phase is much more significant than a basic introduction. The objectives here are:

◆ establish credibility

◆ build connection

◆ take control of the process.

Of course, before meetings, we greet each other, share names where required, sometimes do the 'let's go around the room and introduce ourselves' rituals. On virtual calls, people do the same, plus we have the added benefit of seeing their names on the screen. When giving a presentation, you will often be introduced; however, the context should always be established before introducing yourself formally.

The two steps of the 12-step model we use to establish a strong and credible connection are:

5. Self-intro (earning the right and creating personal connection)

6. Guidelines (the behaviour you want from your audience).

Phase three: Content

In your diagnose phase, you captured some of the content you want to explore in the CPD Hierarchy. That content becomes relevant here.

We have devised four steps in the 12-step model to help you structure your *content* to deliver the outcome. They are:

7. Reintroduce the concept

8. Lay out your principles (use anchoring; we cover this in detail in Chapter 12)

9. Present the details (core content/stories)

10. Summarise by re-emphasising the principles (use the same anchoring points).

Phase four: Call to action

I was coaching Kris, a senior executive, on her upcoming board presentation. The content related to climate change threats and the potential risks to her financial services organisation. The content was clean, supported with punchy examples. As we walked through the design, we realised there was no call to action.

'What is the call to action? What do you want the board to do with the information?' I asked.

'The board just requested an update, and this is it', was her response, 'so there is no call to action.'

Here was a wasted chance for Kris to influence the board to provide better governance. In addition, it was a lost opportunity for her to assert her leadership. It's important to remember that all information has some implication or application for its audience.

In Chapter 2 we asked ourselves 'What is the outcome from the audience's perspective?' The call to action should answer the question: At the end of the meeting what will the audience *do*? As we mentioned in the introduction, influence is designed to shift how people feel, think, behave and what they commit to.

The call to action is fundamental to being influential.

When we get to Step 11 of our 12 steps in Chapter 7, we'll discuss how your framing and content need to lead somewhere — and this is where your call to action is critical.

One step in the 12-step model address the 'what do we do now?' question:

11. Call to action! This includes the ask (if needed) and next steps.

Phase five: Close

The primacy and recency effects state that information presented at the beginning (primacy) and end (recency) of any presentation, meeting or conversation is retained better than information presented in the middle. It relates to how the brain functions, and is a natural cognitive process.

We have often seen communication situations where the close is not well understood by the audience, usually due to poor or unclear design and delivery.

Step 12 wraps up your communication powerfully and effectively supported by a strong close, hence, the final step of the 12-step model is:

12. Strong close.

***

Each of the 12 steps correlates to one of the five phases. In the next chapters you will see how these two models work closely together to structure your communication.

CHAPTER 4
PHASE ONE — CONTEXT

The five phases will be the map of the design work. These phases will become so familiar, it will be like driving a car. As a learner driver, it takes time and practice to achieve competence and confidence. The phases will become as natural as any skill you have mastered where unconscious competence is in play. But, first, we must do the hard work of practising step-by-step.

First impressions

First impressions! We all know how quickly we judge, assess and evaluate each other. We can instinctively mistrust someone within seconds of meeting them despite having no evidence or data to validate the feeling.

The best communicators consciously work on first impressions — not from an egotistic or self-serving point of view, but to create the right conditions for success.

How you start counts. I recently watched some of the Ryder Cup golf tournament played outside Rome. The commentators referred to the opening drive from the first tee. 'If Rory can get this down the middle of the fairway on his opening drive, it will inspire the European team.'

What? How is it possible in a game, where they will collectively be hitting hundreds of shots, that one drive could be of such significance?

The answer is that a strong start sets the tone, creates expectations, and can and does inspire confidence.

We call this *nail the opening* (NTO). In fact, we see the first eight steps as a full NTO, and it takes some work.

Let's work through each of the 12 steps. Have your working scenario handy to revisit as we go.

Step 1: Start strong

Starting strong is the first step in setting the context. The goal of the start strong is to get your audience's attention immediately. The quicker you engage the person, group or audience, the more effective you will be. It's the perfect drive off the first tee.

Here are four ways you can start your communication strong:

1. ask a question

2. use a data point or numbers

3. tell a story

4. use a quote or statement.

Ask a question

A well-considered question, where a response is required, immediately engages people. It also signals to the audience that there is an expectation that they will interact.

Types of questions to open with include:

◆ How many of you ... ?

◆ Does anyone know ... ?

◆ Who can tell me ... ?

For example: 'How many people around this table know what the average cost to process a call from our members at our call centres is? <Pause> This is not rhetorical. I'm sincerely interested in our collective understanding of costs when it comes to connecting with our members. Any ideas?'

Professor Robert Cialdini, in his ground-breaking book *Influence: The psychology of persuasion*,[10] identified a significant aspect of human behaviour called the commitment and consistency pattern.

Psychologically, people are likely to maintain consistency to a commitment they make. For example, why do people continue to support a losing sports team? Why don't they just support the top team that is winning that week? Well, they made a commitment. Failing to stay consistent with that commitment is seen as disloyal.

When someone responds to a question, either verbally or nonverbally, they are making a commitment to participate. They have moved from a neutral, observer position to an active participant. Because of this, they are more likely to stay involved in the conversation.

DESIGN

A well-crafted, thoughtful question is a potent way to start strong. A great example of this is Simon Sinek's TED talk on how great leaders inspire action.[11]

Use a data point or numbers

Using data to start a conversation or presentation is an effective tool that has been used for a long time. The opportunity to build intrigue and interest at the beginning of a conversation or presentation is the tactic.

A presenter shows a PowerPoint slide with three numbers: 24, 9, 12. Nothing else. No context. Just the numbers.

The presenter then says:

> *These numbers identify the challenge we face in cost management. The number that should be of most concern for everyone around this table is the second one, the nine, and this is going to be the focus of our conversation today.*

Everyone will now be assessing and evaluating what the numbers might refer to, achieving the objective of getting the audience's attention.

We saw this beautifully done in 2023 in Dubai at the kick-off for a technology company. Professor Edward Challis walked on stage in front of 600 people. On the screen was one number: 82. He opened with, 'This number tells the story. This is all we need to know as we plan our go-to-market strategy for the year ahead.' Everyone leant in. He had everyone's attention.

Originally, he had a busy, text-based slide that gave away the opportunity to start strong. He took the first draft of the slide, which read, 'A 2022 EY report, which surveyed executives across a range of industries to determine their prioritisation of artificial intelligence and automation in their planning, found that 82% of senior executives considered this a core focus for the future.'

The key number is, of course, 82. Ed turned a research finding into an intriguing start strong.

You can, of course, consider using data points to ask a question, combining the first two start strong elements. 'Can anyone tell me what this number, 82, might refer to when we think about our customers?'

One, or a few, data points and numbers is a powerful way to start strong. For a great example of using numbers for a start strong, watch the TED talk by Hans Rosling called 'Global population growth, box by box'.[12]

Tell a story

We are hardwired for stories. Our brains are designed to make sense of the world around us and we constantly compare previous experiences while imagining possible futures based on the experience of the present.

Stories immediately create context and meaning, while also requiring the audience to use their imaginations to construct the narrative in their own minds as the story unfolds.

However, stories have to be tightly designed and well told. We all know people who tell stories that are dull beyond words, rambling or irrelevant to the context. We will delve deeper into storytelling in Chapter 20.

The key to an effective start strong story is brevity.

Your start strong rolls into relevance (Step 2) so the story needs to logically lead into the 'Why? Frame' or relevance set-up.

DESIGN

You might have seen a politician talk about the time they met someone:

Last week, I was visiting a shopping centre in my electorate, and I met Maggie, a single mother of two girls, and she told me how she is struggling to feed her children. Maggie said, 'last year we would have money left over, now I have to watch every penny. It's exhausting.' This government does not care about people.

The story provided the foundation for the politician to criticise government policy, without having to use data to validate it. The story (whether true or not — it's a politician after all) does all the heavy lifting.

The theme of your story can inspire, provoke, challenge, amuse or intrigue, but the intention of the story is to lead into building a compelling relevance frame. For an example of a start strong using stories, watch Brené Brown speak on 'The power of vulnerability'.[13]

Use a quote or statement

'Insanity is doing the same thing over and over and expecting different results.' This quote is attributed to everyone's favourite physicist, Albert Einstein.

At almost every conference I've attended, this statement or quote has been referenced at some point, often on a slide or simply mentioned by the speaker. This is *not* a start strong. Why? Because you run the risk of it being a cliché or a tired reference. To start strong, you goal is to grab attention. If there is a risk that the audience has heard this before, they may disengage.

However, starting with an appropriate and apposite quote from a customer, an employee, a thought leader or a vox pop can be an excellent bridge into your relevance positioning. We saw this used at a New Zealand conference where the quote used to start a session on staff engagement was: 'Asking our people to work harder is like a farmer asking a flock of sheep to grow more wool.'

It immediately caused people to pause and think. The leader of people and culture attributed the quote to a BBC comedy program, *TV to Go*, and it led to an analysis of the constant demand placed on employees to do more at less cost, with fewer resources, and the implications this has on culture.

Other examples of quotes or statements that cause someone to pause and think include:

DESIGN

> *Corporate culture is the only sustainable competitive advantage that is completely within the control of the entrepreneur.*
>
> David Cummings, co-founder of Pardot

> *Customers will never love a company until the employees love it first.*
>
> Simon Sinek, author and motivational speaker

> *To win in the marketplace you must first win in the workplace.*
>
> Doug Conant, former CEO of Campbell Soup

For an effective example of using quotes in a presentation, watch Elizabeth Gilbert's talk titled, 'Your elusive creative genius'.[14]

Time to work

Think about how you will hook your audience. Craft your opening using one of the techniques here (story, question/statement, data point/numbers, quotes). Which one resonates most for you in the context of your communication plan?

Step 2: Create relevance

If you are in any conversation, meeting or presentation as a participant, there is one foundational question always playing in your mind: 'What's in it for me?' (WIIFM). Self-interest naturally drives most of our behaviour.

Your relevance design addresses this question. We have already done work on this in the diagnosis phase (refer back to Chapter 2 for a refresher).

The golden rule here is: relevance *before* concept.

Most average communicators will introduce the topic, theme or concept first, and then expand on why this might be important, significant or valuable. For example:

Concept: Today I'm going to talk about our Q2 results.

Relevance: This is important is because it will help us understand what went well, where we could have improved and where opportunities are for Q3. Q2 data will ensure we can plan effectively so we all succeed over these next three months.

Now reverse this and note the difference.

Relevance: Q3 awaits us. Today, we will be able to set up foundations for success for all of us in the room. What we will decide today will ensure we can grab opportunities, reduce distractions, focus on the right things and leave no one behind over the next three months. How will we do this? What is the best way we can plan intelligently? That's easy… let's learn from what we already know…

Concept: Today, we are going to look at our Q2 results.

We are all guilty of premature closure. We rush to judgement (or closure) on limited information. This is usually based on previous knowledge or experiences, biases or prejudices, perspectives or beliefs.

Someone might hear 'Q2 results' and immediately 'close' on what this will mean and tune out the following relevance frame.

Relevance *before* concept deepens the context and can unfreeze someone's fixed point of view to allow them to be more receptive to the content or data you are about to share. As my mentor, Marvin Oka, taught me over 35 years ago, 'Don't take a horse to water because they may not drink. First, make the horse thirsty!'

The analysis of appropriate relevance has already been done in your diagnosis. The decision now is to determine how you will 'script' your relevance frame, placing appropriate emphasis on the lever that will work best for the audience you are working with.

Do you use the 'aspirational lever', articulating the possibility of a successful future?

Do you use the 'fear lever', moving people away from risk or uncertainty? In a 2023 national referendum in Australia seeking the inclusion of Indigenous voices into the federal policy setting, the 'No' campaign won by its frantic focus on the 'fear lever', a common tactic in politics.

Do you use the 'personal success lever' to encourage greater performance or commitment?

As we discussed in Chapter 3, and as you considered in your diagnosis, relevance is critical to influencing others.

To engage someone, to get their attention, they must feel that what is being discussed or shared is *worthy* of their attention and energy.

DESIGN

It's the fundamental driver of everything you do in your life. There must be a reason why, even if it seems odd or incomprehensible to you. For example, the 'Why? Frame' of a suicide bomber seems bizarre and antithetical to the instinct to live, yet in their minds, it makes sense.

All you have to do is answer the WIIFM question in your audience's or participants' minds.

> **Time to work**
>
> Use the pain/gain/challenge/ease formula discussed in Chapter 3 to formulate your why. Why does your audience need to know or understand this content?

Step 3: Introduce your concept

You've most likely heard about the book *The subtle art of not giving a f*ck* by Mark Manson.[15] I dare you to not be curious about what this book is about. The provocative title immediately grabs your attention, hinting at a counterintuitive approach to life's problems. If Mark Manson had called his book *Managing life effectively,* it may not have been the ridiculous bestseller it has become.

The concept described in the book title *The tipping point: How little things can make a big difference,* by Malcolm Gladwell,[16] was so effective that it has become a part of our vernacular. The term 'tipping point' has been around since the 1950s, but Malcolm Gladwell popularised it.

Now apply this principle to your concept.

Remember, it's about context. I would not risk giving a board presentation a title like 'Let's make sure we don't screw things up', even though that may be the underlying sentiment. However, something like 'The risks of risk' is more appropriate and intriguing.

Imagine attending a meeting or presentation and what would happen inside your head if you saw one of the following on an opening slide?

- Annual compliance training

- Updated HR policies review

- Data entry best practices

- Workplace safety guidelines

- Employee benefits overview

- IT system upgrade update

- Procurement process changes

While each of the conceptual titles are accurate, they don't have the attention-grabbing element needed to heighten engagement. Rather than expecting everyone to get excited about a presentation on an 'IT system upgrade update', you could try something along the lines of 'Tech revolution: The future of our IT universe'.

'I don't see why I have to come up with snappy, gimmicky titles for my presentations' an insurance executive said to me last year. 'Why can't we just call it what it is and get on with business?'

Fair point. However, if your intention is to profoundly influence, secure attention and create the conditions for full engagement, then the concept description needs to be carefully considered. It's about the audience. What will spark their interest or curiosity versus merely induce compliance and ritual participation?

DESIGN

Remember, understanding the audience's needs and expectations, and crafting the presentation to meet them, is pivotal in delivering content that is engaging and memorable.

And it starts with the concept.

The concept title should be not only captivating, but also give a glimpse into the content, theme or main argument of your communication, message or presentation.

Table 4.1 shows the top three considerations for describing your concept.

Table 4.1: Framework to describe your context

Clarity and relevance	Memorability	Audience appeal
Descriptive: Ensure the title gives a clear idea about the issue or subject you set up in Step 2: create relevance on page 46.	*Catchy:* A title that is catchy, easy to remember and pleasant to say can enhance word-of-mouth value after the meeting or presentation.	*Resonance:* Ensure the title speaks to the pain points, interests or curiosities of your target demographic.
Direct: Avoid being overly cryptic or abstract, so your audience can quickly understand the subject matter.	*Unique:* Ensure that the title stands out.	*Language and tone:* Adopt a language and tone that align with your audience's expectations and preferences.
Examples		
Green dreams: Innovations for a sustainable tomorrow *AI hospitals:* Healing hands, digital minds	*Learning unleashed:* Revolutionising education with technology *Viral visions:* Crafting content in the age of social media	*Digital Darwinism:* Adapt or die *Workforce whirlwind:* Work–work balance?

For your concept to influence, you need to think headline!

Time to work

Write a punchy, memorable title for your communication. Aim for six words or fewer, if possible.

Step 4: Manage the FODs

Have you ever gone into a meeting already thinking, 'This is going to be a waste of time'? Have you attended a virtual meeting thinking, 'I'll have my camera off and get on with real work'? Can you recall sitting in a presentation and within minutes feeling disengaged, or worse, mildly pissed off that you have to listen to the next 45 minutes of stuff?

When was the last time you were in a high-stakes situation and felt almost paralysed by anxiety, wondering if your brain would work and hoping against hope that you would not be asked to say anything?

These all fall into the classic FOD space: fears, objections and doubts.

Managing FODs in every communication context is crucial to effectively convey your message and foster a positive and constructive environment. This ensures your audience feels heard, respected and valued by reducing fears, managing anxiety and diminishing scepticism and doubts.

In 2014, I watched an executive at an airline introduce the structural changes that were going to take place in their engineering department. About 400 people sat in the room and this guy blew it. Seriously.

He did not address any of the glaringly obvious FODs in play. He spoke about business efficiency, the need to reduce costs and waste, and the need to improve performance. The majority of the room were riddled with anxiety about their jobs and their futures. Many were furious that management was implying that they, the engineers and support teams, were ultimately responsible for performance challenges, washing their hands of accountability. They were also aware that restructures in other parts of the airline had been less than successful.

You can guess what happened. Halfway through his presentation, the room erupted, the exec failed to manage the situation, and he was shouted off the stage.

If he had simply addressed the FODs it would have been a very different outcome. He could have said:

> *I know many of us here will be wondering how this could affect you personally. Will this impact my job, my role, my future? We will show you how we will protect everyone's job. And, as I say this, some of you might be thinking, 'Why should we believe you? The passenger services restructure did not go to plan.' And, you are right; we learnt a lot from that process.*
>
> *On Tuesday, one of the pilots said to me, 'I hope you are not going to avoid responsibility like management did with the challenges in engineering — they are the best in the world at what they do.' And she was 100 per cent correct. Our record of engineering*

excellence is world leading. And, as we all know here, we cannot be complacent. I will discuss how management will change and improve as well.

Three paragraphs, three simple statements, would have changed the game.

We will go deep into FOD management to understand how critical this is in creating well-formed conditions for achieving your influence objectives. In the following design work, anticipate that FOD management is built into the entire conversation or presentation. However, managing FODs early in the NTO design is key to creating the right context for success.

DESIGN

FOD management design

FOD management starts with three steps:

1. Make a list

2. Preparation

3. Mind-reading.

MAKE A LIST

Research your audience and identify their concerns. What are the possible fears, objections and doubts that could arise related to your content or the topic under consideration? List them.

Typical concerns could include:

◆ more work

◆ more changes

- loss of something (position/status/resources)

- hidden agendas

- heard this before

- waste of my time

- too expensive

- don't believe you

- precedent (tried this before and it failed)

- I'm too busy for this.

PREPARATION

Formulate well-researched responses and include data to counteract or mitigate potential objections or doubts. For example, if one of the beliefs people have is that an upcoming restructure will be painful, threatening and a source of anxiety, you should craft your communication around addressing those concerns. Research success stories and look for validating data to support your upcoming FOD design.

MIND-READING

We define mind-reading in social and psychological contexts as having a high degree of empathy or perceptiveness, where you can pick up on the subtle nonverbal cues, body language and emotional states of others.

This mind-reading form is based on observation and inference rather than direct access to another individual's thoughts. However, when you use the following mind-reading technique, it shows your audience that you can understand and empathise with the current situation.

Quick example.

You want to buy a new fridge, and you decide to go to an *actual* store. (I know this is unlikely, but work with me.) You walk around looking at different fridges, when the salesperson approaches you and steers you to an expensive unit. Then she says, 'Now you might be thinking, "whoa, this is expensive and outside of my budget".' If she does her job well, you would think, 'Yes, that's exactly what I was thinking.'

What she has done here is raise the objection *before* you, implying she has a way to argue against this limitation.

The goal of mind-reading is to demonstrate your awareness of the person's reality, therefore, you have factored this into your argument, your position or your message.

The basic set-up for mind-reading, therefore, is 'You might be thinking…' but let's get more sophisticated with the technique.

FIRST-PERSON APPROACH

'Now, I *know* what you are thinking…' is a direct approach. You need to be confident in your understanding of your audience's FODs.

'You *might* be thinking…' is a softer, more indirect approach. This is a safer approach with larger audiences.

THIRD-PERSON APPROACH

'Some people think…' is assertive and, therefore, direct.

'Some people *might* think…' is more generalised and indirect.

The third-person approach is often used in journalism as a way of mind-reading stakeholders.

DESIGN

'Minister Forest, a lot of people in your electorate are saying (thinking) that the current government has not delivered on its promise. They are upset and struggling. What do you say to them, minister?'

The 'people are saying' or 'people are thinking' references social proof. This rhetorical device is very common because it works.

FODS MANAGEMENT THROUGHOUT THE COMMUNICATION

One technique you can use is the feel/felt/found approach.

Feel: I understand how you *feel*.

Felt: Others have *felt* the same way.

Found: This is what I (or others) have used as a solution or outcome when addressing this concern.

We use this approach a lot in one-on-one coaching.

It's crucial to approach FODs with genuine respect and a willingness to engage in a constructive dialogue. Addressing these aspects thoughtfully can assist in managing the immediate presentation context and building your reputation as a credible and empathetic communicator.

Remember that the goal is not to 'win' an argument, but to build understanding and rapport with your audience.

Time to work

Using your communication scenario, brainstorm all the fears, objections and doubts that your audience may be feeling. If your example is for a small group, you may need to diagnose FODs for individuals. For each FOD, write down a mind-reading response using the construct 'You might be thinking' or 'Some people think'.

CHAPTER 5

PHASE
TWO — CONNECTION

The first four steps established the context. We now move to building connection.

Step 5: Self-intro

Self-intro is about two things: credibility and connection

In many communication contexts, your audience will already know you: for example, having a team ops meeting, a performance conversation or presenting to a group you work with. They know who you are. They know your name.

So, is Step 5 necessary in all communication contexts? In a word, yes.

Self-intro is *not* about your name. It's about establishing or deepening your credibility and building a connection with your audience.

Log onto a Zoom meeting or MS Teams call and, of course, you are doing the social 'how are you?' stuff. Your name is right there on the screen or you might be introduced by someone.

So, why do we still need to do the self-intro step, and why is it so late in the process? Some people think it's rude not to introduce themselves earlier.

Remember it is always, always about the audience. And, in particular, the audience experience.

The start strong, relevance, concept and FODs flow builds interest and curiosity, and keeps the audience hooked as they gradually understand the context. Because you are doing this, you are demonstrating your competence and credibility without having to give a CV or title.

Watch any TED talk. The speaker never introduces themselves first. In a presentation context, like a conference or an event, the biographical information is available beforehand anyway.

Finally, because you have built a compelling context, they are genuinely interested in who you are.

Designing the self-intro

For an effective self-intro, you should break down your approach into three sections:

1. My name is: _____

2. My background is: _____

3. My role today is: _____

1. MY NAME IS ...

You may not always need to answer this first question. If you are unsure, you could say, 'I think I have met most of you, but just in case, my name is ...'

I recall a Spinal Cord Forum in early 2003 where Christopher Reeve was the keynote speaker (see figure 5.1). As MC, I introduced him, and he wheeled himself onto the stage in front of an audience of over 2000 people.

Figure 5.1: Christopher Reeve crafted a compelling self-intro
Source: © Chris McGrath / Getty Images

After opening remarks, where he powerfully shared the life-altering effects of a horse-riding accident, he said the following. 'My name is Christopher Reeve. I was an actor. Some of you may have seen me in a few movies. I'm now a researcher and educator. I'm an advocate for the power of the human spirit.'

What was so powerful was his humility. While everyone in the room knew who he was, he didn't assume it. The feeling of connection in the room became palpable; the energy became hyper-present. It was an extraordinary moment I will never forget.

Your name is your brand. It's significant and not something to throw away. How many times have you met someone at an event or meeting, and they've said 'Hello, my name is brrrrrrrrrrrrr' so quickly that you could not get it? It feels awkward to ask again. So, we politely shake hands and smile. Their name is lost.

SAYING YOUR NAME

If it is appropriate to introduce yourself by name, then say your name slowly and deliberately. Of course, we know how the famous line 'My name is Bond. James Bond' goes in that movie franchise. It's a moment we wait for in each movie. James delivers his name seriously, sincerely.

We are not advocating that you copy the James Bond pattern; however, we can learn from this.

A pattern that works well is to say your first name distinctly, then pause before saying your surname in a slightly lower tone (see figure 5.2).

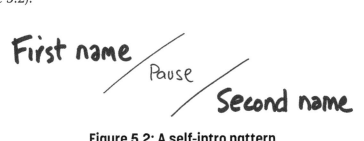

Figure 5.2: A self-intro pattern

This will feel very theatrical, almost contrived, when you first do it; however, remember it's for the benefit of the audience. They will remember your name.

If you are fortunate enough to have a distinctive name, you may need to spend time ensuring everyone understands it. I recall a Microsoft executive introduced himself at an event in Boston: 'My name is Harsha Joseph Chaminda Randeny', and he said it fast, without pauses 'HarshaJosephChamindaRandeny'. He then paused, smiled, and said, 'And I bet none of you could repeat that. We Sri Lankans love our names, so please call me Joseph. Joseph <pause> Randeny.' I still remember it.

2. MY BACKGROUND IS ...

When designing your self-intro, remember it is all about context. What will establish you as credible for *this* audience?

The time you spend on this will be defined by context too, of course. A presentation can give you further scope to incorporate stories to deepen the audience's understanding of who you are and what you bring to the table.

Something as simple as, 'In my 15 years working in this industry, across four different cities, I have faced this issue many times' immediately evokes a sense of authority and breadth.

'To give you some background ... ' is a standard way of leading into a background reveal. Avoid providing a CV list. Highlight the experience, knowledge and achievements that validate your right to present or share the information you are about to share.

The *connection* element is to reveal something personal that humanises you.

This was brilliantly done by a new executive general manager who was holding his first town hall with the 600 people in his business. He has an incredible business reputation and people were a little intimidated by his commanding energy and international experience. When he arrived at the self-intro step, he created a connection with the following: 'At breakfast this morning, my nine-year-old daughter, my eldest, asked me what I was doing today, so I told her I was giving a big speech — this town hall — and she asked me, "Dad, are you nervous?" My four children all looked at me waiting for my answer, and I had to say ... "yup, a little".'

In a few words he revealed so much about himself. He's a father of four children under the age of ten; he has breakfast with them rather than rushing out of the house; and he made himself vulnerable and human, revealing his nervousness. He connected. Powerfully.

3. MY ROLE TODAYS IS...

How you define your role in the meeting sets the expectations.

'I will be leading *this meeting.'*

'My role today is to facilitate *our discussion.'*

'My role today is to present *the overview, and to manage the Q&A that follows.'*

'Today I will support *our team in outlining the plans for Q4.'*

You could be in a coordination, leader, facilitator or presenter role. The label defines your role and your audience will adjust accordingly. Make it explicit.

A strong self-intro convinces the audience that they are in safe hands.

Time to work

Now it's your turn to write your self-intro following the pattern of:

My name is: _____

My background is: _____

My role today is: _____

Give some thought to how you will build a connection through your credibility and being relatable.

Step 6: Guidelines

Have you ever sat in a meeting where people are constantly looking at their phones? It's distracting, often disrespectful, and usually extends meetings because points have to be revisited when someone misses something.

In the absence of a guideline around phone etiquette, people will make up their own rules. The purpose of the guidelines phase is to explicitly state the rules of behaviour for the session you are involved in. Ensuring the rules are understood and agreed to reinforces your authority and credibility. The transition into the guidelines is simple:

'Let's get a few guidelines down to ensure this session works for all of us.'

'Can we agree to a few guidelines to ensure a productive meeting?'

'Okay, here are the rules of the game for our workshop today.'

'Could I ask that we agree to a couple of things to make the best use of our time today?'

There are four guideline areas:

1. Technology

2. Q&A

3. Notes

4. Participation

Technology

Do you suffer from bandwidth separation anxiety? It's a thing. Nomophobia is the irrational fear of being without a mobile phone. We probably all have a bit of this.

In 2007, Steve Jobs launched the first iPhone. We all know how this has shaped the way we work, live and play. The ubiquity and dependence on our devices intrude into every communication context and, at times, this needs to be managed to support a better, more effective experience for people.

In January 2018, I was attending a regional kick-off meeting in Singapore for a large technology company. The room was packed with about 2300 employees flown in from 14 countries. The energy in the room was all buzz and fizz. Kick offs are a big deal. An expensive big deal.

Out comes the MC, full of spark and zest. He does the 'are we all excited?' stuff before announcing the arrival of a senior exec who had flown in all the way from the United States.

He comes onto the stage. Quite formal in manner. Stands behind the podium thing and does a classic opening. Not a start strong.

I was standing at the back of the room watching all this. Within 30 seconds of the beginning of his opening address, I watched hundreds and hundreds of heads fall forward as they accessed their phones. Technology won the day. The phones were more interesting than the speaker.

You need to decide how to manage this when setting guidelines. A simple request not to look at phones will be largely ignored. You need to be explicit about the reason and value of putting phones away.

One way we do this in our work is something like: 'I notice some phones on the table and already in hands. Could we approach this meeting with full commitment and attention? I'm sure you would agree that minimising distraction and listening to each other will produce the best results. Can I ask that we put our phones away? Would that be okay?' It works.

You might be using technology for polling and other interactivity, however, you need to encourage the appropriate use of technology.

Q&A

Questions are always in play and you need to decide how this will be managed in your design.

We have all seen meetings and presentations fall apart because there were no specific rules or guidelines on the Q&A component. Think about a presenter who, seven minutes into her delivery, is interrupted by a question, which she chooses to answer, which leads to another question, then a comment and, before she knows it, she has lost control of the presentation.

However, sometimes open discussion from the start might best serve the outcome and purpose of the communication event.

Q&A guidelines establish the rules of the game. Here are some examples:

I will walk through the presentation for about 15 minutes, most likely less, and I know there are a lot of questions, so can we wait until I've delivered the overview and we can get down to some discussion and analysis?

Let's make this a conversation, as I go through the report, please ask any questions or make comments as we go along. I will manage the process to ensure we don't go too far off the main road and stay on theme.

We have allocated 20 minutes for Q&A. Can we please keep our questions short, and without too much commentary, to ensure we can get as many questions as possible.

DESIGN

As I talk about the solution we recommend, you might find yourself disagreeing early in the piece, please stay with me as I outline the full picture, and you will see that we have considered everyone's concerns and then we can go into discussion and questions.

Managing questions is a sophisticated skill, and this is covered in detail in Chapter 19.

Notes, handouts, documents

Many internal meetings will focus on data, research, documents and reports. These are often sent ahead of time for analysis in the meeting. When pitching, there are often slides or information that can be provided either as a hard copy or emailed after the event. In workshops or training contexts, participants will take notes and expect handouts to support the process.

Providing guidance on how notes, handouts and documents will be managed helps everyone to understand the rules of engagement and, importantly, demonstrates your authority and control of the session.

TRAPS FOR YOUNG PLAYERS

If a report or pre-read document has been provided, do not go through the information in detail. Too many times we have heard 'I'll take the document as read' and then they go through the document or report in detail. Your role is to provide a high-level summary before moving into analysis, questions and discussion. Here are some examples:

As you have received the pack and detailed report, let's use this time to consider any thoughts, reflections or concerns you have. I will go through the concept and principles to ensure we are aligned and then get into discussion.

As I outline the strategy, please follow using the handout provided.

We will work through the deck together. You have the printed deck in front of you. Could I please ask that we stay focused on the page I'm referring to and not to leap ahead despite the temptation. It will ensure we are not distracted or miss the set-up to explain the data.

There is no need to take notes, we will send you the deck straight after this presentation.

There is a lot of detail that we need to go through. It will be slow, hard work. We need to ensure there is nothing we miss or fail to understand.

Failing to give explicit guidance can lead to disengagement, confusion or low-value compliance.

Participation

Think about the times you have attended a communication event, and you were unsure on what you were supposed to do? The tendency to go into reflective observer mode in these instances will be high. In the absence of guidelines on how to participate, the safest posture to take is to be neutral and opt for listening mode.

Look, we all sit in meetings all the time, and it's easy to get into automatic pilot mode. Can I ask that we shift gears and bring our full attention and energy to the conversation today? So, if you are feeling kind of neutral right now, can you decide to be present and let's make this time worthwhile for everyone here.

In October 2023, I was presenting to 250-plus property managers. The venue was very wide and the energy was a bit fractured. The MC tried hard to grab people's attention, but the energy was still scattered as he introduced me to the stage. When I got to the guidelines, I started with this: 'Before we get into the content, can I ask every one of you, "how have you shown up today?" How many of you need more time before you decide to be present? What can you do now to commit your attention to what this day holds for you and your colleagues?'

Approaching the participation guideline through questions changed the dynamic in the room immediately. At the break, one of the participants came up to me and said, 'Thank you for your session. I arrived feeling so tired, I have two children under three, and was not ready for today. You really woke me up and I decided to be here fully. Thank you.'

All it took was a well-designed participation guideline.

How long?

Having gone through this guidelines framework, you might be thinking, this could take a lot of time, leading to the question, 'How long should the guidelines take?'

The answer is: *it depends.*

The guidelines piece could be as simple as this:

> *Before we get into the work, can we all agree that phones distract us and each other. Could you please put your phones away? Is that okay with everyone? Good. (technology)*

> *I'm going to spend about 20 minutes going through the data, and then we will have a robust and lively conversation for 30 minutes, so please save your questions until we get to the discussion phase. (Q&A)*

> *I will send you a copy of the slides I'm about to go through so no need to take notes. (notes, handouts, documents)*

So, let's all get our heads into the game, leaving any issues outside the door, so we can fully commit to our time together now. (participation)

Done. 30 seconds.

However, you may have a difficult audience, with lots of competing issues and agendas, and the potential for conflict or disagreement. Not only does your FOD management have to be on point, but your guidelines around respect and consideration to alternative points of view need to be explicit. In some contexts, we can spend 15 minutes on guidelines alone, sometimes longer. On longer training programs, over days, we can spend up to 30 minutes to ensure full appreciation and understanding of expectations and rules of the game.

Time to work

Consider the preferred behaviour you would like to see when you deliver your specific communication. Draft some guidelines for your participants by considering the following:

- Phones/tech: Be adamant about the rules here. If you are not explicit, people will not comply.

- Questions: Do you want questions after the presentation/pitch or during?

- Notes/handouts: Should people take notes? Will you leave behind a report/deck/handout?

- Participation: Will it be a table discussion, group work, brainstorming, etc?

CHAPTER 6
PHASE THREE — CONTENT

Step 7: Reintroduce the concept

The concept has already been set up in the context steps; however, the connection steps have taken attention away from the content.

To bring your audience's attention back to the event, Step 7 is to remind them of the concept. For example:

We are now ready to get into the work. Let's remind ourselves again that we are here to focus on **<concept>**, *so let's go deeper.*

Step 8: Lay out your principles

Think about principles as the chapters of a book. To return to the *7 Habits of Highly Successful People*, each habit was a chapter. Very simple to navigate.

When audiences or participants get lost, it's because the structure of the communication is unclear. How often, when a presenter is on slide 10, have you wondered, 'What are they talking about?' Their content lacks reference to a guiding *principle* and, sometimes, lacks an overarching *concept*.

In verbal communication, we suggest the number of principles should be no more than six. If you were a participant in a presentation and the speaker said, 'There are 23 points I will cover in this presentation...' you would most likely tune out. Too much. If, on the other hand, a presenter says, 'We are going to look at four key areas in the strategy', you would be more likely to stay engaged.

Each principle is a subheading to the concept and needs to be punchy and brief. For example:

> *Let's look at how we will win with our go-to-market strategy.* [**concept**] *There are four elements we need to all get behind. Firstly, get segmentation right — at the moment we are all over the place.* [**principle one**] *Secondly, it's all about the ADS — increasing the average deal size.* [**principle two**] *Thirdly, we are not pitching, we are telling our story.* [**principle three**] *And finally, marketing magic... some exciting news here.* [**principle four**]

So, there we have it...

Think of your design like layers:

The first layer is relevance.

The second layer is the concept.

The third layer is the principles.

Finally, there are details and data.

This provides the necessary scaffolding for the listener to follow your communication with ease.

In a meeting, if you have a point to make, give it a CPD structure, for example:

> *There are three things I want to say in response to the risk report. First: timeliness. Second: communication to stakeholders. Third: one major concern. Let me start with timeliness.*

When we get to delivery, we will look at the skill of anchoring in Chapter 12 to make your words more impactful and memorable.

Step 9: Present details

The skill of designing the detail is to apply the packing principle. If you are packing for an overseas holiday, pack everything you think you need, then take out 50 per cent. We overpack communication with too much content.

Georgia Murch, a colleague and friend of ours, puts out a monthly newsletter to her database of clients. She rarely uses more than 300 words, and her newsletters are punchy, deeply informative and memorable.

The rule of thumb is, if you have trouble remembering your own content, then your audience has no chance. Under each principle (Step 8), map out the key details relevant to concept and aligned with your relevance frame (Step 2). Ideally, you will add at least one story, example or real-world scenario to illustrate the implications and applications of the content.

Time to work

Map out the detail for your communication plan for each principle you have identified (Step 8). Provide the details, including data, a story, an example, a process, an analogy or an activity for each principle. You'll need these for the next step.

Step 10: Summarise by re-emphasising the principles

Summarising the content by returning to the principles elegantly integrates your content and serves as a natural transition into the call to action.

Let's revisit what we have just covered. Remember the four pillars to the strategy we have just explored. First, our segmentation is on the money: we know our customers and market.

Secondly, we all agree, average deal size changes the game for everyone.

We then looked at our story, and we must all practice this with each other. And finally, marketing magic is all about the support we have wrapped around our go to market.

This is a quick summary. Avoid elaboration or the temptation to drop into more detail at this point.

CHAPTER 7

PHASE FOUR – CALL TO ACTION

Step 11: Call to action (the ask/next steps)

The design is to ensure we answer the question: what is the outcome from the audience's perspective?

At the end of your communication, what will the audience feel, think, do and commit to? So far, we have addressed the *feel* aspect through relevance (Step 2) and context setting (Step 3). What the audience will *think* is clearly addressed with the delivery of your content, structured using the CPD Hierarchy framework from page 26.

Now we get to the *do* part. Influence is the ability to change the way people feel, think and behave. The behaviour is linked to the call to action.

You might be thinking that not all communication has a call to action. What if you are just updating a group on a project, or simply informing them of some change? We argue that any and all communication has some implication and application. Even if it is minor. 'Please share this information with your teams at your next meeting' is a basic call to action. 'I will follow up next week to see if you need further clarity or explanation' now moves you into the *commit to* phase of the outcome.

The call to action can be complex and detailed, and therefore, needs conscious thought when you are designing your instructions or guidance to ensure clarity and understanding. The call to action is often poorly designed and poorly delivered. As it comes towards the end of your communication, the temptation to rush this is high. Think how often the same stuff is discussed in meetings. There is so much talk, talk, talk, talk. Action is the goal of influence.

There is a middle-sized technology company that is currently growing rapidly. It's grabbing AI and automation with both hands and helping companies stay relevant and competitive. We have seen the impact one person has made to this business in Europe. His focus is always action, action, action. For example, there had been a year or so of discussion and analysis about the workload account managers were carrying — some with up to 100 customers. The data showed that some customers were unhappy with the quality of service and lag times in responses to requests. What could they do about this? Reports, debates, discussions and many, many meetings were conducted to try and address the challenge. In comes the new leader of the Europe sector. In week one he tells the sales teams: you can only have 20 customers. Any customers below a certain threshold do not have a dedicated sales person; they are managed by a support team. As you can imagine, there was initial pushback, heat and noise. This quickly changed as he used a story to illustrate how this has worked before. He introduced the Louis Vuitton handbag story: 'Do you want to sell one handbag for $10 000 or 1000 handbags at $10 each? We have been selling Louis Vuitton quality at Kmart prices.' This one example caught on immediately. He influenced the entire workforce to understand quality, focus and value. That quarter Europe exceeded its budget for the first time in three years. Boom.

Influential people change behaviour. Knowledge does not change anything. Everyone knows how to eat healthily. Everyone knows how to save money. We all know stuff. Turning stuff into action, into behaviour, is the key. This is the ultimate goal of success.

Building in accountability, support and follow up becomes an imperative.

My brother owns a wellness and health centre called Be Well. The target market is people over 40 who want to ensure a long, healthy and flexible life and a functional, pain-free old age. Every gym and health centre in the world kind of promises the same thing.

What makes Be Well different is that an agreement is made with every member about what they will commit to in order to ensure what they learn and do is done regularly and consistently. If a member does not show up, they are asked if they would like a telephone call, a text or email to check in. This simple contract not only ensures attendance, but the members feel cared for and realise that the promises made are not simply marketing stuff.

This is the essence of 'commit to' and needs to be built into your call to action design.

Time to work

Think about your call to action. What do you want your audience to think, feel or do? What are you asking them to do and what are the next steps? How are you going to follow up or show your commitment to (commit to) your audience or team after the communication has been delivered?

DESIGN

CHAPTER 8
PHASE FIVE — CLOSE

Step 12: Strong close

Your strong opening created the space to make a quick positive impression from the first moment. In a live context, a start strong is conveyed by how you sit in a meeting, how you walk onto a stage, and of course, the first words you say.

Your *strong close* is as important as your start strong.

As human beings, we are profoundly affected by the primacy/recency phenomenon (see page 38). We are likely to remember the start of something as well as the end.

Reflect on how many meetings or presentations have ended in a weak or rushed way. We call this the Enya ending — the energy seems to 'fade away, fade away, fade away ...'

The close strong has four requirements:

1. Future pace the implications and applications of what people have just heard.

2. Tie back to your start strong (question, data point, story, quote).

3. Link back to the relevance and Why? Frame.

4. Thank the audience, participants or individual. Keep it simple.

Let's look at each of these in more detail.

1. Future pacing

Future pacing is a profound influence technique and we're going to devote a bit of time to it. It's a concept that originates from the field of neuro-linguistic programming and has found applications in various domains, including, of course, corporate communication. Future pacing was originally used to reinforce positive behaviour and outcomes by getting individuals to 'experience' the positive outcomes in their mind before they actually occur.

We future pace all the time.

Nervousness and anxiety are a product of future pacing. Imagine something that hasn't happened yet, like a major presentation, and see everything going wrong — forgetting your content, the audience looking bored or hostile, your boss staring at you with rage — and, yes, you will feel deep anxiety. And all of this is happening in your mind. Worrying is future pacing negative outcomes.

Is it useful to worry? To future pace negative outcomes? Yes, of course. Anything that is risky or has an element of danger needs negative future pacing. However, it is important to balance this with future pacing success.

Sports psychology is a major subscriber of future pacing. I heard one of Australia's greatest Olympians, the cyclist Anna Meares, being interviewed after achieving one of her 23 world records: 'We had the time we wanted on the wall of the gym. I just knew that this was the time I would achieve. And we did it.'

So, how can you use future pacing in your business?

STRATEGIC PLANNING

So much time in corporate comms is spent discussing strategy — either in constructing the plan or, more often, communicating the plan to the various stakeholders.

When designing your close strong, you want your audience visualising the successful implementation of a strategy, identifying potential hurdles, understanding the steps needed to achieve goals and fostering a sense of commitment to the vision.

In July 2023, at a Health Organisation Leadership Conference on the Gold Coast, I saw the leader do this very powerfully. She laid out the plan in the content session with the usual boxes and arrows, however, her close strong brought it all together.

> *When you get back to work on Monday, you will call your team together and share the slides I've just shown you. You will explain that the next seven months will be challenging. Do not sugar coat this. Our people are smart and are not taken in by sugar-coated words. What they will do is respect the transparency and honesty. What will happen is that our vision to be the best in the world at patient-centred care — the best in the world — will lift their heads and stir their passion.*

DESIGN

CHANGE MANAGEMENT

This is universal. Every single organisation, business and company is always undergoing change, especially as technology becomes more and more significant in how we work, live and play.

Most people future pace change as a negative.

'This will mean more work.'

'I'm going to lose my job.'

'This means less security, less resources, more demand.'

These, and statements like these, are negative future pacing. This needs to be balanced in your close strong design. Future pacing can assist stakeholders in visualising the benefits of the change. By focusing on the *positive* future outcomes, resistance can be minimised, and buy-in can be enhanced.

People of influence push against the negative future pacing habits of the majority. They hold onto the possible. Steve Jobs, through his sheer conviction and commitment to design excellence, changed the mind of analysts who predicted failure, shareholders who sold their Apple stock in truckloads, employees who were looking elsewhere for work and customers who were not convinced. In 2023, Apple's market value was close to US $3 trillion. This is bigger than the entire economies of countries like Germany, Japan and the United Kingdom. Steve Jobs embedded change as a normal process — which it is.

Every entrepreneur has to positively future pace in order to sustain and maintain themselves and their teams when dealing with the uncertainty, volatility and the unrelenting pressure to build something from scratch.

This does not mean you will automatically succeed if you are positive about the future, the goal and the outcome; it just means you will be more effective in managing the journey.

TRAINING AND DEVELOPMENT

This is our bread and butter. We constantly use future pacing in our training sessions, especially when introducing new tools, technologies or methods. By helping participants visualise their successful use and the benefits of the methods and tools they are using, we can accelerate adoption and reduce anxiety.

SALES AND MARKETING

Sales professionals use future pacing to help potential clients visualise the benefits of a product or service. This visualisation leads to a more profound emotional connection to the product or service and increases the likelihood of a purchase. All advertising is built around the future pacing concept.

LIMITATIONS AND CONSIDERATIONS

No model is completely foolproof, and like any strategy, you need to tailor it to your audience and be aware of where it may not serve your intention. Some things you should think about with future pacing include the following.

Over-optimism: Without a grounded approach, future pacing can lead to overly optimistic projections that may not consider realistic challenges. The risk here is you come across as unbelievable or inauthentic. We saw one leader make extravagant claims about earning potential in his organisation. No one in the room believed him. The data did not support his ambition. He came across as foolish.

Requires skilful facilitation: This is why a close strong design has to be deeply considered. Ineffective facilitation can lead to shallow visualisations that don't provide the depth needed for genuine insight.

DESIGN

Step into the hearts, minds, bodies and shoes of the people you are seeking to influence. Your future pacing descriptions must be real, based on their reality and their model of the world.

Cultural considerations: The effectiveness of future pacing might vary based on cultural differences in the perception of time, future orientation and visualisation practices. This will be key in the diagnose phase of the Triple D model (see page xxii for a refresher).

FINAL THOUGHTS ON FUTURE PACING

As you apply future pacing to your communications, you will discover that it is a powerful tool used to inspire action, facilitate change and drive commitment. As your design and delivery improves, you will find that you can profoundly affect how people are feeling and thinking. You will see them shifting their mindset and attitude. The more you do this, the more skilled you will become. As the corporate landscape becomes more volatile and uncertain, your skills at future pacing will serve as a guide in supporting your audiences, participants and colleagues towards success.

2. Tie back to your start strong

Looping back to your start is one of the most powerful experiences in storytelling.

A leader from a major bank in Australia was presenting to a large forum at the Sydney Convention Centre in 2017. His start strong was a story of a conversation with a bank customer, Julie, who found herself and her two young daughters in a refuge for women experiencing domestic violence. She had contacted the bank asking to work at nights as a cleaner, not for pay, but to meet her mortgage obligations. He told this story in a very quiet, undemonstrative way, before going on to his concept of corporate social responsibility to victims of domestic violence.

His strong close was to conclude his story on how the bank supported Julie in her time of need.

The audience of 2000 spoke of no presentation other than this one after the event.

3. Link back to the relevance and Why? Frame

This is a simple reminder of the Why? Frame from page xx, and of hitting your key messages.

Revisit your Why? Frame, and the messages you included in your 'Relevance' step. You need to remind your audience of the 'why' case to reanimate their interest and provide the fuel needed for the call to action.

And that is why we need to do this. Our competitors are ahead, and we need to overtake. Now.

This will protect our customers and employees against the scourge of cyber-attack.

You can see the necessity of making this investment now rather than waiting.

This will demonstrate our duty of care in supporting our teams in doing their jobs better.

4. Thank you

As always, this is about context. In most situations, you will design a thank you to simply acknowledge the time and attention of the people you are communicating with. However, there will be times when you need to thank those involved in organisation of the event. Conferences are one example of this.

DESIGN

Keep it simple. The audience knows that this is the close and the energy will reflect that. You've established your strong close in the looping reference to your start strong and relevance, and your audience will expect a tight conclusion.

When presenting, we recommend standing at the centre of the stage. Hands clasped. Body still. 'Thank you for your time, attention and energy today.' Small bow. Done.

In a meeting, picking up papers or a notebook and tapping it on the table as you thank everyone for attendance serves as a clear conclusion.

In a one-to-one, a simple acknowledgement will suffice.

Time to work

Design a strong close for your communication. Don't forget the four steps:

1. Future pace: set a strong, realistic vision for the future.

2. Tie back to your start strong: link back to your number, story or quote.

3. Link back to the relevance and Why? Frame: Remind your audience why your call to action is critical.

4. Thank the audience, participants, or individual. Keep it simple.

Using the 12 steps to design your conversations, meetings and presentations will, with practice and consistent use, become second nature. Time to move on to delivery.

In summary

♦ **Phase 1: Context**

1. Start strong: Grab the attention/interest of the audience.

2. Create relevance: Why will this audience need/want to know this?

3. Introduce your concept: This is your topic.

4. Manage the FODs: Fears, objections and doubts.

♦ **Phase 2: Connection**

5. Self-intro: Earning the right to speak.

6. Guidelines: What behaviour do you want from the audience?

♦ **Phase 3: Content**

7. Reintroduce the concept: Bring the topic to the attention of your audience.

8. Lay out the principles: Use anchoring, left to right from the audience perspective.

9. Present details: The core content/stories.

10. Summarise by re-emphasising the principles: Remind the audience of what they have heard.

DESIGN

◆ **Phase 4: Call to action**

11. The call to action: Bring it back to the next steps using anchoring and the timeline.

◆ **Phase 5: Close**

12. Strong close: Loop back to the start strong and relevance steps.

PART III
DELIVERY

Give ten people you know a five-minute script on leadership and four slides. Give them a few days to prep, and then film each one delivering the information. What will be the outcome?

We suspect you will experience ten different approaches to the identical script and slides. The reason we know this is because it's not about the content, it's about the delivery.

You may have attended a meeting, and made a thoughtful, important point. And nobody noticed. It's like you simply made some noise. Four minutes later someone else makes more or less the same point, and everyone reacts positively. Same idea, more or less the same words, very different response. How does this happen?

Have you been guilty of sitting on a Teams or Zoom call and you simply tune out some people? Not a deliberate act on your part, you simply zone out. Much of this reinforces the importance of ensuring that it is not just what you say, it's how you say it.

Of course, other factors like status, credibility and subject matter do play their part. If the CEO bounced into your meeting unexpectedly and offered some thoughts, you would most likely listen attentively, regardless of her communication methodology. Status has a value.

However, we are going to put other factors aside, and focus deeply on the methodology of *how* you deliver *what* you designed.

Over the years, we have researched everything associated with work-based communication across hundreds of organisations in many different countries. We've deconstructed TED talks, famous speeches, world-class comedians and performers. We even spent time with Larry Moss, watching how he coached actors in deepening their method.

We have broken down everything to do with work-based communication into six discrete, yet connected categories, and we will delve deeply into each of these with techniques, examples and exercises for you to practise and apply.

We call this framework PAVERS®.

CHAPTER 9
THE POWER OF PAVERS®

The PAVERS® technique provides the elements to make your content design come to life, and have the influence you are looking for (see figure 9.1).

Figure 9.1: The PAVERS® technique
The PAVERS® technique is a registered trademark
of Altmore International Pty Ltd

Watch people in a social situation communicating with each other: a family gathering, a pub or a party, having a meal in a restaurant. What is apparent is human interaction is full of movement, gestures to describe and bring words life, vocal variety, energy, interaction and exchange, and inevitably, the exchange of stories. It's how we communicate.

We incorporate each element of PAVERS in almost every communication context you care to name.

Observe someone on a mobile phone in a public place. Why do they gesture even though they cannot be seen? Simply observing their body language and facial expressions would give you some idea of the type of conversation they are having.

A sports crowd is fascinating.

Source: © Phil Noble / PA Images / Alamy Stock Photo

We all know what happened here ...

What will immediately elevate your influence ability is to consciously practise and apply the elements of PAVERS in every communication situation. A coaching client illustrated this for me in our final session in November 2022.

> *What astounded me was the simple use of gestures. I was simply unaware how abrupt and overly forceful I was being with my hands. I literally shut people down, when my intention was to ask for their point of view. Being the eldest of four brothers, I had unconsciously employed controlling gestures in my way of communicating. I'm now much more comfortable in being open, inviting and considerate in the way I use my body and gestures. My effectiveness has gone through the roof.*

The first step of PAVERS is *physiology*, which covers everything to do with how you use your body:

◆ posture

◆ gestures

◆ movement

◆ facial expressions.

The next step covers the *auditory*, meaning everything to do with voice and language:

◆ pitch

◆ pace

◆ projection

◆ pauses.

In corporate communication, it's not just what you say, it's how you say it. Your voice carries the soul of the message.

DELIVERY

When we talk about *visual aids* it covers tools such as slides, whiteboards, flipcharts and the imagination. Some principles to consider include:

- less is more

- show don't tell

- reveal equals revelation

- alternatives to PowerPoint.

As Steve Jobs said, 'People who know what they're talking about don't need PowerPoint.'

The next step is *energy*, and energy is everything. It's your:

- passion, commitment, congruency

- energetic signature

- emotional wake.

Variety is the key with energy. Angela Ahrendts, CEO of Burberry, shares a moving exploration of human energy.[17] We are all reservoirs of energy, and we are sharing our energy every moment of our lives. Are we doing this with clean intention?

The next step focuses on *relationships*, the exchange and interaction that occurs between people:

- relentless respect

- interaction

- the power of names

- language of inclusivity.

Every communication is founded on the relationships between the players in the room: live or virtual. Your ability to influence will be based on how they connect with you.

Lastly, we focus on *story*. We are all storytellers; we just sometimes forget that we are. We have already touched on the importance of storytelling, but in the context of PAVERS, we will look at:

◆   magic formula stories

◆   story types

◆   story library

◆   storytelling.

We are a product of story. Your culture, family of origin, background, gender, socioeconomic factors, even your postcode contribute to the story that is you. We are hardwired for story. It is the ultimate way we learn anything. Story is the source of meaning, the reference point for morality, the foundation of your worldview.

Story is the most profound influence tool we have in communication at work, but it's the one tool that is often left in the tool box.

DELIVERY

CHAPTER 10

PHYSIOLOGY

Have you ever watched an old silent movie? While there were some captions you could read to hold the story together, those actors relied entirely on their physiology to convey the story, the emotion, the jeopardy, the humour and the action. Charlie Chaplin became one of the world's most famous actors using his physical expression alone.

We are always communicating with our bodies, even when we are alone. Have you ever felt down or depleted and your body turns into a heavy sack that you drag around the house?

Have you been sitting alone at work, getting ready for an important presentation, and you move around to shed any nervous energy?

Your body plays a crucial role in all communication, shaping both the delivery and interpretation of messages.

Understanding the components of *posture, gestures, movement* and *facial expression* — all elements of your physiology — will offer profound insights into the dynamics of work communication and enhance the effectiveness of all your interactions (see figure 10.1, overleaf).

Figure 10.1: Mastering your physiology

Amy Cuddy in her TED Talk on Presence simply talked about posture.[18] Over 50 million people have watched her deliver the message that good posture enhances your presence.

Posture

If you are reading this in a public place, look around you. What do you notice about the people you can see? What is their posture communicating about how they are feeling, their mental state? Walk down a street and observe. Who is confident? Who is exhausted? Who is scared? Who is self-conscious? Can you spot a tourist?

Our posture conveys information about us all the time. And no more importantly than at work.

We can all spot a negative person, simply by the way they show up. It's reflected in their posture first, their energy second, their demeanour third. Posture sets the tone for entire interactions. A firm handshake, maintained eye contact and an upright posture can give the impression of confidence and competence.

We are often unaware of our posture, let alone in control of it, leading to our emotions dictating our postural position. Someone feels nervous and they can immediately *look* nervous. Their posture will reflect their anxiety. Your posture can also affect how you are perceived by others. For example, people who adopt expansive, open postures (like standing tall with shoulders back) are often perceived as more confident, competent and authoritative than those with closed, slouched postures.

What if we could control our posture? The answer is we can. Your posture can and will influence how you feel. Research by Amy Cuddy[18] and colleagues found that adopting 'power poses' (open, expansive postures) can increase feelings of confidence and decrease feelings of stress. You can literally choose the posture you want — you can do it now. If you are seated, then adjust your posture to sit with an attitude of confidence. What did you need to do? Straighten your back? Lift your head a little? Square your shoulders?

Being mindful of posture can aid in stress regulation, especially during challenging or confrontational situations at work. This can be especially useful before high-pressure situations, such as presentations or interviews.

With the rise of remote work and virtual meetings, the role of posture has become even more critical. People can still pick up on postural cues through video, which can shape perceptions of engagement, attentiveness and professionalism. Good posture during virtual meetings can also help prevent physical strain and fatigue, a common complaint with extended screen time.

There are cultural considerations to be aware of though. We have been working with a Scandinavian company that has undergone a change in leadership, taking on a number of executives from the United States. On many occasions, I have heard the Scandinavian employees complaining about the strut and 'arrogance' of the Americans, which has created tension and mistrust. 'They walk in here like they own the place.'

The American executives were surprised by this reaction as they felt they were 'being themselves'. The professional communicator, the professional person of influence, knows when to adjust to context, and to adjust to audience. Part of your development of your postural awareness skills is, as always, context.

We refer to the practice as 'the physiology of excellence'. Practise walking confidently wherever you go. Become conscious of your posture. Imagine a cable tied to the top of your head, ever so slightly pulling up. This lengthens your spine, improves your posture, retrains your physiology. Take a look at recent photos. What does your posture say about you?

Virtual physiology

Post-COVID we have all adapted to using Zoom, Teams, GoogleChat and the like. We have seen colleagues sitting in various rooms, with various backgrounds and camera angles. What can make an immediate difference is how you consciously use your physiology to create a positive and effective on-screen presence.

On your next virtual call where most people have their cameras on, take notice of your colleagues. How many of them look slumped or distorted because of camera angles? How many appear disinterested, distracted or disengaged? You are making assessments of how they appear of camera.

How do you appear? Are you slumped? Do you occupy the whole screen or are you 'shrunk' into the bottom half? No one wants to look at people's foreheads or up their noses.

Now, try changing your posture, and make sure the camera is at eye level. Ensure that your head and shoulders occupy most of the space. Most importantly, look at the camera when you speak — it creates virtual eye contact (see figure 10.2, below, and figure 10.3, overleaf).

DELIVERY

LOOK at the CAMERA 80° of the time
Both on your seat — And on your feet

Figure 10.2: Camera at eye height

Figure 10.3: Ideal virtual screen; look at the camera

Ideally, for important meetings and presentations, you should stand, and this means elevating your computer — a stand-up desk is ideal. If you are serious about being a person of influence and impact, encourage your employer to buy you a standing desk or make the investment yourself.

Standing keeps your energy up and allows you to move left to right, towards and away from the camera. This immediately ensures you can incorporate movement and gestures more naturally. Movement on screen also draws attention (more on this in Chapter 12).

Check in with yourself

One last important aspect of postural awareness is *emotional regulation*. The best communicators can stay calm in tense conversations or high-stakes meetings.

Understanding your physiological responses can help you regulate your emotions during stressful situations, such as negotiations. For example, being aware of your rising heart rate or shallow breathing can help you know when to pause and recentre.

The good thing about posture is that you can practice your physiology of excellence every day. Walk confidently. Stand with respect. Sit with high attention. What is your posture of curiosity? Find energetic differences in your posture, your gait and in your sitting positions.

DELIVERY

CHAPTER 11
GESTURES

'Whenever I'm presenting, I never know what to do with my hands.' We hear this often.

Our response is always the same: 'Where else in your life is this a problem? Are you walking down the corridor thinking, what do I do with my hands?'

Gestures are powerful communication tools, and we know that when people use gestures, they do it quite naturally. Again, observe people in social situations and notice how naturally expressive people are in using gestures unselfconsciously.

Handshakes

Let's start by looking at one of the most interesting uses of hands: the handshake. This is an almost universal form of greeting, with artistic depictions of this behaviour dating back to Ancient Greece. While it is now a form of greeting, it began as a way to check for weapons (if the person you were greeting was armed, they may be carrying a knife strapped to their forearm).

These days, the handshake has become a standard and widely accepted form of greeting in many cultures around the world. It's used in professional settings to greet, leave, thank, congratulate or seal an agreement. The meaning can vary depending on the context and the culture, but it generally symbolises goodwill, respect and openness.

A few months ago, I was running a program in Budapest, Hungary. Such a beautiful city. One of the participants from England is a determined, ambitious guy. He walked up with his tall, confident gait, put out his hand and said, 'Good to see you again, Colin'. We shook hands. This time I was ready. His handshake was one of those crushing, dominance moves. Full on alpha.

I immediately asked him if this is how he normally shook hands with people. He looked a little surprised. 'Why do you ask?' 'Because you are overcompensating with your handshake. It's too much.' He had no idea. He explained that his Yorkshire father had always said, 'Have a firm handshake, son. Always have a firm handshake.'

He had almost everything working for him with regard to posture, however, he needed to temper his handshake. He has since done so, and he now makes a confident first impression rather than coming across as trying too hard.

It might seem odd to say that shaking hands is a skill, however, a poor handshake can diminish your credibility, status and impression before you even say a word. You may think there's nothing to a handshake, but there are methods you need to be aware of to shake hands properly.

When do you shake hands? When another person is speaking or introducing you, wait for them to finish speaking and then offer your hand. It is here you stand tall, or at least mirror the posture of the person you are shaking hands with. There are some cultural dynamics to be aware of, particularly with regards to firmness of grip. In Western cultures, a firm, confident grip is positively received. In the Middle East and most Asian cultures, a more gentle, but still a little firm grip is more polite.

It goes without saying that if you're seated, always, always stand before shaking someone else's hand. This shows courtesy and puts you at the same level as the other person. Avoid the dominance stuff where you extend your hand palm down, forcing the other person into a submissive response. This alpha stuff is obvious and disrespectful. You may have been on the receiving end of some of these moves. They become almost comical. Politicians in opposition play these games, including pulling the person towards them to show 'big ape' energy. Tedious stuff.

In summary, you want your handshake to convey quiet confidence and respect.

Gestures in the workplace

In the work context, people tend to be much more conservative in their use of gestures, both in meetings and presentations. If this is you, you are missing a key opportunity to influence.

There is a conventional formality that is applied in most work contexts, where the focus is on the content, not the expression of the content. Hence, gestural containment. Of course, there is a time and place for everything, including times where gestures need to be reduced or used sparingly.

Gestures play a crucial role in reinforcing verbal communication, adding emphasis, and enhancing the overall clarity and impact of a message. In the workplace, using gestures effectively can significantly enhance one's influence, both face-to-face and online.

DELIVERY

We will start with what gestures do to support your communication before we get into the how.

The most obvious place to start is that gestures enhance *clarity* and *emphasis*. Gestures can help highlight important points or data, making the message more memorable. For example, counting off points on your fingers or using hand movements to show the size or scale of something can help emphasise and clarify. Consider saying something like, 'We are planning some big changes'. What does this mean? How big is big? Let your hands give your audience some sense of scale (see figure 11.1).

Figure 11.1: How big is big?
Source: © Wayhome Studio/Adobe Stock

Movement attracts attention. No surprise here. If someone is standing at a lectern delivering a traditional speech, and a moth starts to fly around behind them, the entire audience would be transfixed on the moth. Its unpredictable, sporadic movement would demand the attention of everyone in the room, except the poor speaker of course.

Gestures can achieve a similar effect by *engaging* the audience. Dynamic communicators often use gestures. By varying their gestures, they can keep listeners' attention and make their presentations more engaging (see figure 11.2). For example, if someone is talking about the future and points to their left, the future (from the audience's perspective) is identified.

Figure 11.2: The future is to your left
Source: © Thanasak/Adobe Stock

Comfortable and natural use of gestures creates an interesting impression; it conveys *confidence*. We have already looked at posture, and that coupled with gestural expression and movement will project confidence. The key is to control your use of gestures.

Someone who is nervous or anxious may use gestures, but they are fidgety, unconscious and distracting. A common one we see is hand wringing. Or playing with a ring on a finger. These 'tells' are hands in motion without control or intent, conveying nervousness and low confidence.

The objective is to take control of your hands. Think about this as gestural vocabulary. This is *not* sign language. Sign languages are a unique way of communicating for the deaf community and are complex, textured and mostly non-literal ways of expressing language physically. Thinking about gestures as a way of communicating or reinforcing verbal messages is the name of the game here.

Synchronised gestures that align with what's being said can make the verbal message more potent. For instance, moving one's hand upwards when talking about growth can visually reinforce the message. Of course, we provide non-verbal feedback all the time. Simple nods, thumbs up, hands clapping and the like provide immediate feedback and encouragement without interrupting the flow of a discussion.

On virtual calls there is a banquet of emojis that are designed to do exactly that (see figure 11.3).

Figure 11.3: Signal your emoji

Watch a parent with a child, and notice how much of the parental communication is gestural along with facial expression. The same dynamic occurs in meetings. A simple glance at a colleague could translate to 'What the hell is she talking about?'

Gestures can also regulate and help manage the flow of a conversation. For example, raising one's hand to interject or using a hand to signal someone to continue speaking can help regulate turn-taking in discussions. Later, we will look at some universal ways of calming people down, or directing the conversational traffic.

Gestures can also help your audience understand complex ideas. In 2007, we were working with a group of scientists from the

Coca-Cola organisation. One scientist told me that if they could reduce the weight of plastic bottles by 1 gram, this would save billions of dollars in plastic bottle manufacturing. When they explained this, it was complicated stuff about microns, atoms and the like. One of the participants got the gestures idea, and illustrated his abstract concept by blowing up the structure of an atom with big gestures. 'Imagine this is the nucleus of an atom', he said, 'holding' an imaginary football in his hands, 'and over here are the electrons', he walked 2 metres away and used his hands to illustrate imaginary tennis balls, before going on to explain how they could shave microns off the thickness of a plastic water bottle by electron manipulation. We all got it. No visual aids other than gestures.

Finally, having a rich gestural vocabulary, with a natural, effortless use of hands will enhance your personal presence. Effective use of gestures can make someone appear more charismatic, particularly in situations where personal influence is essential, such as negotiations, chairing a tough meeting, delivering a keynote or leading a team.

Let's get into specifics.

'It just doesn't feel natural to use my hands; it feels like I'm performing. Surely the content is what counts, not all the theatrics?' is a comment I received from a business leader in Hong Kong in 2016. He was a successful guy, self-made, independently wealthy. He enjoyed the challenge of work, and had a very analytical, data-focused approach to work and communication. He was a willing student though. When he realised that communication was not about him, but about his audience, he embraced gestures as a critical communication tool. He is now a global CEO whose on-stage presence and delivery have become one his most talked-about qualities.

Learning gestural skills and building a gestural vocabulary takes work. It will feel odd and contrived at first. The self-conscious part of your brain will kick in suggesting you go back to safe neutrality.

DELIVERY

This is the newsreader archetype — very little animation. Of course, if you are a sports reader or weather person, go for your life.

Types of gestures

There are two types of gestures: those that *illustrate*, and those that *facilitate*.

GESTURES THAT ILLUSTRATE

Gestures can demonstrate scale, direction, growth, shape, height, distance and so on. We all use illustrative gestures all the time. The amount of academic research into the use of gestures, gestural types, gestural variability and cultural differences is immense. We would encourage your own research into this.

A classic example of this is the game of charades. This game requires players to use a whole range of gestures to illustrate a book or movie title, with players often using their whole body to convey meaning.

The starting point to developing gestures to illustrate is a technique called *big gestures* (see figure 11.4).

Figure 11.4: Big gestures

Big gestures *underline significant points or ideas.* A sweeping hand movement or a pointed finger can emphasise the importance of a particular topic or statistic. This helps in reinforcing the weight of the message you're delivering. If you are talking about significant growth, sweeping your left arm up and pointing makes this idea real in the minds of the listener, it demonstrates conviction.

Time to work

Let's start with an exercise. Pick a story, maybe something that happened recently. It could be as simple as grocery shopping, hanging with friends, playing with your kids in the backyard. Record yourself or, better still, get someone to record you, telling the story *without any movement* or gestures for about 30 seconds. Then record again, but this time you are telling the story while being *fully animated*, deliberately exaggerating every gesture and movement.

Watch both videos back. What do you notice? Which video is instantly more engaging? What do you notice about your voice? If you were sitting in an audience, which version of the same story would grab your attention?

DELIVERY

Invariably, when we run this exercise, most people think they are being wildly expressive, almost comically so. In fact, the supposed exaggeration is not as big as they think it is, and instead looks appropriate to the audience and brings the story to life.

Storytelling is a good place to start understanding the effect and benefits of expanded and expressive gestures; however, does this apply to everyday work content? In a word, yes.

Big gestures, when used tactically, are a powerful influence tool.

To illustrate this, we'll start with *attention* and *retention.* We are all overloaded with information and distractions, and this can make it challenging to capture your audience's attention. Big gestures can command an audience's attention immediately. When presenting a new idea or pitching a product, a dramatic gesture can underscore a point and make it more memorable. People tend to recall visually stimulating events more than monotone speeches.

In work settings, we all know that communication can sometimes be sterile, and gestures can add a human touch, *making the message more relatable.* That fist pump is instantly recognisable as excitement or victory. Open arms suggest inclusivity, welcome, a question. Using gestures in this way makes you more impactful, more influential.

We worked with a manager in the fast-moving consumer goods world, groceries and stuff, who was very uncomfortable with presenting. Anna loved a lectern. It gave her something to cling on to as she delivered her content in a monotone, with no movement. She wanted to change this, and big gestures is where she started. After lots of practice, and a bunch of courage, she walked up to deliver her usual monthly report to her team. The lectern stood ready. Anna did her usual routine of placing papers on the lectern, introducing her topic on change. Then she did something that transfixed the room.

In a loud voice (very unlike her), she said, 'And if I'm asking for change, then I must change!' She stepped away from the lectern, away from her notes, strode to the middle of the stage and said, 'This requires all of us to think big!' She threw her arms apart, 'and to push the past behind us', using her hands like a bulldozer to push stuff away, 'and we must all commit to this today!' making a fist.

She got immediate applause. Not to mention a fully engaged, and frankly amazed, group of people. They had never seen Anna so passionate, so engaging, so real.

When we debriefed later, Anna described how liberating it was to express herself through her physiology. 'The weird thing is, I'm naturally physically expressive, but I've limited myself over the years because I thought work communication had to be very formal. I've been boring people for years. Never again.'

Finally, one very effective use of big gestures is to *interrupt the pattern of expectation*. Meetings and presentations can be tedious. By integrating big gestures, you can break the monotony, re-engage the audience, and inject energy into the room.

At a recent strategy planning workshop, the energy in the room was flatlining. The facilitator, Tim, suddenly shouted, 'Wait! Wait, wait … we have made a *huge* error.' Everyone in the room looked up, startled. Tim was standing with his arms wide, 'Does anyone know what we have forgotten?' he said as he started to pace around the room. Energy spiked through everyone, people looked bewildered, but they were fully engaged. 'We forgot to have our afternoon break. See you all back here in 15 minutes.' Laughter and relief. This is a big gesture move. It interrupts the pattern, snaps people back into attention and creates respite.

However, while big gestures can be effective, they must be used judiciously and authentically. Overuse of illustrative gestures can come off as theatrical or insincere, undermining the message and the credibility of you, the communicator. Also, cultural sensitivity is crucial; a gesture that's appreciated in one culture might be offensive or misunderstood in another. Always be aware of your audience and the context in which you're communicating.

GESTURES TO FACILITATE

When facilitating a meeting, discussion or presentation, the gestures you use to facilitate are different, and they are critical in communicating influence. We will look at four ways to facilitate

DELIVERY

using gestures to support your words in work-based communication. These are to:

1. Invite

2. Control

3. Reflect

4. Direct.

1. INVITE

Communication is always about participation and relationships. We *invite* people to a meeting. You are *invited* to the conference or presentation. The tacit agreement in welcoming and acknowledging people's attendance is that you are *inviting* everyone to participate and pay attention. During a meeting, we can *invite* people to ask questions or make comments. You get the point.

The gesture of invitation is simple: open hands, palms facing up (see figure 11.5).

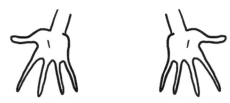

Figure 11.5: A gesture of invitation

The *invite gesture* of showing one's palms can convey honesty and openness, helping build trust and credibility with the audience. Open palms show you are safe and welcoming.

Use this gesture when offering an opinion or a thought contributing to a discussion. In the early stages of a negotiation, this gesture demonstrates that you are open to discussion and willing to listen.

The invite gesture is effective and useful when used appropriately; however, there is downside to the invite gesture. It is often overused and has become a default gesture in work communication, and there are some good reasons for this.

Why? Because it is safe. If you have an opinion, the open hands indicate an offering, no push, no directness. The open palms also give you an out, 'it was just a suggestion'. There are times when this gesture dilutes or compromises the strength of your conviction or the firmness of your opinion. You will witness many conversations where open hands cause the conversation to go on and on, or worse, where the opinion you proffer is not taken seriously.

'I don't know how many times, after a meeting, I feel I was not heard, or simply talked over', is something we hear time and time again.

This is followed by predictable analysis of alphas dominating, gender issues in play or status dynamics. Of course, these are sometimes in play, but take ownership of the response. If you are being talked over, or your opinion is being discounted, it may be you. In other words, it's not *what* you are saying, it's *how* you are saying it. If you come across as imploring, overusing the invite gesture, this could be interpreted as lacking conviction or even confidence. If someone is trying to be adamant and commanding, the invite gesture is not the go-to gestural choice, as you will discover when we discuss the next gesture: control.

Use the invite gesture when:

◆ greeting people

◆ welcoming and acknowledging

◆ offering ideas or suggestions

◆ demonstrating openness and receptivity

DELIVERY

- inviting questions or comments

- demonstrating willingness to go further

- demonstrating 'I don't know' (with shrug)

- encouraging

- acknowledging

- supporting openness and vulnerability.

If you use the invite gesture and state, 'That's my final offer!' who is going to believe you?

Contrast this with our next gesture: control.

2. CONTROL

The *control gesture* carries more authority and is more decisive. Using your hands in the palms down position carries more conviction and strength (see figure 11.6). Saying 'That's my final offer!' while using this gesture is believable.

Figure 11.6: The control gesture

This gesture is also used to pacify. We will instinctively use the control gesture when someone is getting too heated or emotions are starting to escalate.

In March 2012, we were running a workshop in Johannesburg, doing a deep analysis on a struggling company. Things were getting heated. The founder and owner of the business was clearly agitated, and his displeasure was targeted at the CEO. The usual stuff: glowering looks, eye rolling and general huffiness. Then he exploded: 'If only you could do your job!' My co-facilitator on this workshop, Erica, immediately stood up, walked over to the founder, hands flat, palms down and said calmly but assertively, 'Paul, stop. Come with me', before turning and walking out of the meeting room. Paul followed. Figure 11.7 is what timely control looks like.

Figure 11.7: The control gesture can be used to calm
Source: © Yay Images/Adobe Stock

The control gesture is also universal. Every culture uses it with the same intent: to control the situation.

For example, using these gestures at the end of a presentation can convey vastly different meanings.

Invite gesture = please ask.

Control gesture = we are done.

Use the control gesture when:

- asserting a strong position or statement

- concluding a discussion

- closing a meeting

◆ ending a conversation

◆ transitioning to next agenda item

◆ calming a person or situation

◆ indicating something is non-negotiable (flight attendants use control gestures all the time)

◆ reducing tension or to mollify

◆ checking 'are we all done?' (e.g., before the gavel comes down)

◆ closing down an unproductive line of discussion.

There are times when a situation is complex, people are divided, there is a variety of opinion and things may be drifting. This next gesture, again universal, aligns with one of world's most famous statues (see figure 11.8).

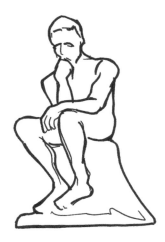

Figure 11.8: Rodin's *The Thinker*

3. REFLECT

Influence is the art of causing someone to change how they feel, behave and *think*. Shifting someone's mental models, or providing insight or input that might change their minds, is a sophisticated process. Human beings can be notoriously stubborn with fixed opinions and views, often without the burden of knowledge or facts.

Adopting a thoughtful posture, with your hand to your chin, conveys a calm, considered presence (see figure 11.9). The *reflect gesture* is the second-most-common gesture used in meetings after the invite gesture. Much of the communication in the workplace deals with analysis, data, decision-making and judgement, so no surprise that reason, logic and a 'cool head' are the order of the day.

Figure 11.9: The reflect gesture

Similar to the control gesture, the adoption of reflect can shift the emotional energy in a room. An HR manager shared the following with us:

I discovered the power of the reflect gesture during a tense discussion. We were dealing with the awful process of downsizing and having to make hard decisions that would deeply impact the lives of many of our colleagues and employees. There was a lot of emotion in the room. I saw it was time to turn down the heat. I sat back, adopted the thinker/reflect posture, slowed my voice down and said, 'Okay, let's pause for a moment. This is a difficult process for all of us. Let's think about what we are required to do. Let's reflect on the fact that this has been done before. Let's learn from what we know.' Immediately, the room calmed. I visibly saw people get into a more thoughtful state of mind. The power of the reflect mode was, well, extraordinary.'

To be clear, the gesture does not mean you literally have to touch your chin — for some of us, this simply looks awkward. The intention is to shift the energy to the head, to adopt a thoughtful posture, supported by the gesture.

What you will notice is that this gesture will cause you to look up and take a deeper breath. It's an unconscious response to the gesture alone. The breath calms your system while bringing your attention from your body to your brain.

Use the reflect gesture when:

- needing to shift the emotional energy in the room

- making a point thoughtfully

- listening to someone, particularly when they are asking questions

- pausing ('let me think about this ...' allowing time to reflect before responding)

- shifting from story back to content and data

- making a point with gravitas

- transitioning to next agenda item or next phase of a presentation/conversation

- negotiating: this gesture can indicate that you are questioning the other's position.

The reflect gesture, like all gestures, needs to be used consciously. Some people have this gestural style as a default, but it can dampen energy as it locks you into one communication style. Variety of gestures is the name of the game. If someone is 'stuck' in the reflect mode, they can come across as too academic or too dispassionate.

The final gestural style is one that needs to be used carefully.

4. DIRECT

No surprises, this is one of the strongest, most assertive and, at times, aggressive gestures (see figure 11.10).

Figure 11.10: The direct gesture

Before we oversimplify and assume the direct gesture is used predominantly in argumentative or accusatory situations, this gesture can also simply point something out, direct someone's attention to something on a slide or point to an imaginary future. The purpose of this gesture is, as described, to direct.

The finger pointing that occurs in arguments or fierce debates correlates with a metaphoric weapon — a pistol, knife or sword — and does escalate emotion and energy. Watch any political debate and you will witness intractable opponents shouting and pointing. It's theatre.

In work-based conversations, we advocate the softer direct gesture of the extended open hand. It still carries assertive weight with less threat (see figure 11.11, overleaf).

Figure 11.11: An open hand is assertive but not confronting

Use the direct gesture when:

◆ emphasising strongly

◆ directing attention

◆ acknowledging someone ('That's a great point, Chris.')

◆ delegating

◆ allocating tasks (at the end of meetings)

◆ facilitating a discussion ('We will hear from Angela first, then we will go to Lee')

◆ prioritising ('The most important point we all need to know is … ')

◆ checking for understanding ('Does everyone know what they have to do?')

◆ managing timelines (past/present/future: 'Remember where we were just three months ago?')

WHEN *NOT* TO USE THE DIRECT GESTURE

Where there is a situation of high emotional potential, the direct gesture will exacerbate things. In these situations, we recommend you opt for the control or reflect gestures.

We had a staff member accuse another of bullying behaviour. These are always difficult because the accusation implies guilt. One person is accusing, the other is defensive, and often there is little objective evidence. Our guidance is always no pointing! In these conversations, the moment the accusing finger emerges, we move from conversation to conflict. As the mediator, I have to be super vigilant that the direct gesture is not used to attack or blame.

Gestures to facilitate help manage conversational flow, the energy in the room, and the style of interaction you seek. Learning when and where to use invite, control, reflect and direct gestures becomes an essential part of your influencing skill.

There are times when we can let the hands do the talking.

Final thoughts on gestures

While gestures can be powerful tools for influence, they need to be used judiciously. If you overuse or rely solely on gestures, it can detract from the message. It's also essential to ensure that your gestures align with your words or they can confuse or mislead the audience. Cultural awareness is crucial. A positive or neutral gesture in one culture might be offensive in another.

Ultimately, gestures should feel natural and authentic. With practice, one can learn to harness the power of gestures to enhance influence in the workplace. It takes conscious practice.

DELIVERY

CHAPTER 12
MOVEMENT

Having explored posture and gestures as elements of physiology, let's now explore the full body in movement.

Again, we have been exposed to people stuck behind lecterns, with their bodies hidden, hands gripping the lectern sides and the often-tedious experience that follows. You can use a lectern well though, and movement is essential to do this effectively.

The simple principle is this: movement facilitates attention. Think back to the fluttering moth example on page 108.

Movement plays a critical role in communication and your ability to influence. As we have already discovered, the subtle and overt physical gestures we use can significantly impact the clarity, effectiveness and emotional impact of our messages.

'How can I move when I'm sitting in a meeting, or stuck in a Teams or Zoom call? There is no room to move, or even a reason!' This is something we hear often. Movement is still critical in effective influence, and movement is possible both on your seat and on your feet.

We will incorporate gestures into physical movement; however, let's start with understanding the benefits of controlled and deliberate movement in your communication. There are differences between seat and feet. The difference between standing and sitting is significant, and this includes both live and virtual situations.

As a case in point, all our virtual workshops and programs are delivered standing. All our facilitators move deliberately to support the messages, create visual interest and, ultimately, engage the audience. It creates a dynamic focus. Similar to gestures, full body movement achieves a number of benefits:

- holding attention

- emphasising points

- expressing emotion

- reinforcing your words

- creating significance

- managing time orientation.

The list goes on. Let's explore more with the power of anchoring.

Anchoring

Anchoring is a powerful concept from neuro-linguistic programming that revolves around the idea that certain stimuli (the 'anchors') can trigger specific states or emotions in individuals (see figure 12.1).

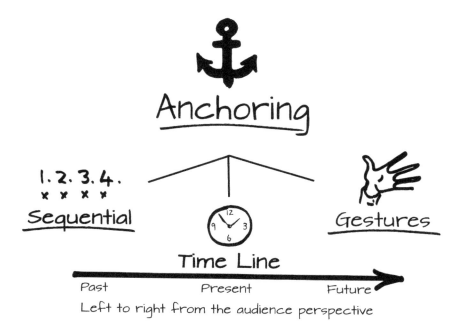

Figure 12.1: The anatomy of anchoring

Once an anchor is established, you can use it to evoke desired states or emotions at will. There are many: images, music, smells, sounds, tastes. Have you ever walked into a place and the smell of cooking or a certain scent brings on a rush of memories? Have you heard a song and been instantly transported back to school, your first love, maybe your childhood?

Here, in Australia, we have terrible fires and often you will hear a distraught owner of house looking at the ruins saying, 'We have

DELIVERY

lost everything, including all our photograph albums.' Looking at your own photos triggers memory and emotion, particularly of lost loved ones.

The stimulus, the photo, triggers a memory, and linked to that memory is emotion. Powerful stuff.

But photos are not memories — they are *anchors* to your memories. When you see a photograph, you are taken back in time to that event, that moment in your family history, or are reminded of certain people. In other words, the photograph is a trigger to the stored memory. That memory is now anchored to that photograph. After all, a photograph is nothing more than an image on a piece of paper. It's what's anchored, or associated, with that image where the story lies. This is why looking at other people's photographs is so boring.

The word 'trigger' is now used extensively when people take offence, get upset or find themselves emotionally bent by what someone said, showed or wrote. In Melbourne, Australia, anything that has Nazi insignia, including the extended arm salute, is banned, because those symbols and actions are anchored to horrific times and awful memories.

You might be asking, how is anchoring applied in influence and work communication?

We will focus on *physical anchoring* or movement. There are a lot of therapeutic applications of anchoring; for example, in reducing phobias and traumatising anchors, however, we will focus on the physiological applications for effective communication only.

In work contexts, such as meetings and presentations, the strategic use of anchoring can help enhance communication, facilitate understanding and manage group dynamics more effectively.

We will delve deeper into three areas of physiological anchoring:

1. sequential

2. timeline

3. gestural.

Sequential anchoring

In most workplaces, the amount of data, information and sheer volume of content can be overwhelming. Our experience of most corporate presentations, for example, is that the deluge of data is simply not taken in by most of the audience. We have previously floated the idea that content is the refuge of the insecure. One of our clients shared this with us.

> *I asked Clive to share his presentation for the upcoming QBR [quarterly business review] with me and he had 99 slides. I showed him how to apply CPD Hierarchy and suggested he identify no more than three core messages to set up the QBR. He could share the slide deck of 99 slides after the QBR but not during the QBR. Then I taught him sequential anchoring. It was a game changer for Clive.*

Let's use this example to illustrate how sequential anchoring applies in the *delivery*. In a classic QBR, the following areas (principles) are covered:

- past quarter performance against full-year goals

- strategic opportunities and challenges

- planning for next quarter.

This is captured in a CPD map as illustrated in figure 12.2 (overleaf).

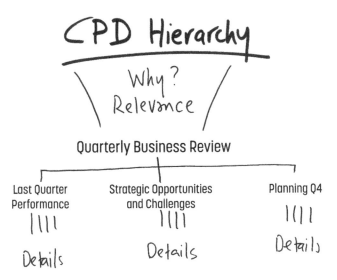

Figure 12.2: Mapping a quarterly business review with the CPD Hierarchy

In the delivery of this content, you outline the three principles in a sequence: first, you cover off the last quarter performance; second, you delve into strategic opportunities and challenges; and third, you move on to planning Q4.

As you read this, you are obviously reading left to right, across the page. The idea is to deliver this in the same way — left to right from the audience's perspective.

If you are standing, you would physically move from your right to your left, physically anchoring the points on the floor or on the stage. Seated at a table, you would emphasise each principle in a line in front of you, from your right to your left.

The key to using physical anchoring in this way is to focus on the sequence, whether that is four steps, three phases, seven pillars, or the six elements of PAVERS®. The sequence gives you the opportunity to anchor your audience between each step.

By moving from your right to your left, the audience obviously views the steps as from their left to their right, which further anchors the points. Most languages are read from left to right, so it's natural that we consume information by reading left to right. Seeing content laid out in this manner helps your audience encode it into their memory. Another point on cultural context, if you are communicating in Arabic or Hebrew, for example, then you would anchor content from your left to right to mirror the direction those languages are read.

Does this really make a difference? Yes. Influence happens below the person's level of awareness and sequential anchoring connects with natural cognitive processing, thereby anchoring the content in the minds of the audience.

The same methodology is applied in Teams and Zoom meetings or conversations. Just make sure your camera is not on mirror view. Try this in your next conversation or your next meeting.

'There are two points I want to make. First...' use your right hand in a direct gesture to anchor point one.

'And my second point is...' use your left hand to anchor point two.

It will seem weird at first, counterintuitive even, because it is. It will take time to cement the habit of communicating in the opposite direction to your own bias, however, your audience, unaware of what you are doing, will follow your content flow more closely and find it easier to remember.

If you are standing, then you physically move on the floor or stage. The bigger the space, the more you can move. The secondary benefit is that it conveys the impression of 'owning the stage', which also helps inspire confidence in your audience (see figure 12.3, overleaf).

Last Quarter
Performance

Opportunities
& Challenges

Planning Q4

Figure 12.3: Examples of sequential anchoring

We have already touched on this in our sequential anchoring, but let's understand how we anchor *time* through movement.

Timeline anchoring

Ask someone what their COVID experience was like and observe their body language. Most will look to their left, or even point or extend their hands to their left, their past, as they describe their experience. As we've discovered, we are hardwired to operate on a left to right orientation unless you were raised speaking languages written right to left.

We do this all the time. We reference our past to make sense of the present in anticipation of the future.

From a delivery point of view, anchoring time on a left to right continuum from the audience perspective intuitively makes sense for them.

Similar to sequential anchoring, the timeline is linked to content relating to temporal references.

'Last month, we faced some difficult challenges.' [Your right]

'Today, we have pulled through and are in a good place.' [Middle]

'Giving us a good foundation for the next three months.' [Your left]

We use time anchoring to support the audience to recognise the temporal context of your content.

When on your feet, physically move or point to link the time references, as you would with sequential anchoring. If you are seated, use the table to anchor time in a live meeting. Simply point or use the table as a mini 'stage' to locate the anchor points. In virtual meetings, use gestures in a similar way, to achieve the same result.

Much of the time, particularly when PowerPoint slides are used, the information is graphed and time is indicated. Your job is simply to follow the growth curves or date progression as it is depicted on the screen.

From now on, you will be stunned to notice how many communicators use time indicators that are intuitive to them in direction, but backward for the audience. Even if there is a slide of a growth curve on the screen, they will tend to point in the opposite direction.

Again, this is subtle stuff. Most audiences are oblivious to timeline management. As you develop your anchoring skills and awareness, your ability to engage your audience will be enhanced through the natural use of sequencing and timeline management.

DELIVERY

At a sales kick-off meeting in Dubai in early 2023, we were told six salespeople would share customer success stories. Our job was to rehearse their five-minute presentations to be given to the 1000-strong audience. Our first meeting was a hugely noisy meet-and-greet drinks session the night before, where we discovered they each had PowerPoint decks, some with 14 slides. Much to their consternation, they discovered that they could only use one slide with the customer's name and two data points, and that we would meet at 7 am for rehearsal. The following morning, some of them looked like they were still recovering from the night before.

During rehearsal, we only worked on timeline anchoring, using the entire stage, starting with their history with the customer, what the current status was and what the projected future looked like.

They learnt anchoring in real time and nailed it. One of the presenters from Leeds, England, got a standing ovation. She was amazed. 'I have never presented without PowerPoint slides before. I was terrified and hardly slept. But now? How liberating!'

Finally, let's look at how gestures can be used to anchor ideas or principles.

Gestural anchoring

Someone cuts you off in traffic. You blare the horn with justifiable anger. The offending driver might respond with a gesture that, ironically, offends you. These insulting gestures are gestural anchors, and every culture has its set of inappropriate gestures. For example, in Vietnam, never cross your fingers, as in 'fingers crossed' for good luck — it is considered profoundly rude.

Every sport has umpiring gestures to ensure spectators know what's happening. Famously, in cricket, the simple raising of an index finger by an umpire is what every batter dreads and every bowler hopes for.

As we have already learnt in Chapter 11, illustrative gestures give a visual reference to things, such as dimension, scale, growth, reach, etc. Having a specific gesture to support your sequential anchoring adds further reinforcement to the meaning of your principles or ideas.

For example, if I talk about significant growth, I need to have a gesture that illustrates this graphically. Not just some little hand movement, but a big gesture showing a rise in growth towards the future. An illustrative gesture for technology could be simply 'drawing' a square and using a typing gesture.

Start with the principles step of your CPD Hierarchy to develop gestural range.

We can see the growth opportunity for next year.

The second point we need to understand is ...

Think where we were a year ago.

What's the plan for the future?

The change is significant ...

Let's think about this further ...

You might be wondering why this is necessary ...

This has been driving us all a little nuts. It's frustrating.

As I see it, we have two options here (the upper hand represents the option you prefer)

There is nothing overly dramatic in these gestural choices. What they do achieve is reinforcement of the message you are conveying.

Your ambition is to develop your gestural vocabulary. Most people won't even notice that you are consciously practicing and using gestures.

Every meeting, conversation and presentation is an opportunity to build your anchoring proficiency in sequential, timeline and gestural anchoring. It will become second nature in no time.

Time to look at your face.

CHAPTER 13
FACIAL
EXPRESSION

We *all* make rapid judgements about people based on their facial expressions. Of course, we do. If someone walks towards you frowning and looking threatening, you react appropriately and get out of their way.

Dr Alexander Todorov, a Princeton University psychologist, conducted significant research on first impressions.[19] One of his most noteworthy studies is on how people judge political candidates based solely on their facial appearances. Here's the catch — the people making the assessments did not know the faces they were shown were people running for office.

Todorov showed pairs of portraits to roughly 1000 people and asked them to rate the competence of each person. Competence. That was it. Not likeability, authenticity, attractiveness or any other criteria. The 1000 people simply had to choose, based on a facial expression in a photo, who they felt was the most competent. Remember, these were candidates for the United States House and Senate in 2000, 2002 and 2004.

I suspect you've already guessed the outcome of this research. The ones rated as competent had a 70 per cent win rate in the elections. Even looking at the faces for as little as one second yielded the same result, and a snap judgement generally identified the winners and losers.

The implication of this research for us is we need to be conscious of our facial expressions. Our faces are constantly communicating—whether we intend to or not.

I work with audiences large and small all the time. Since COVID, I've delivered to over 1000 people in virtual workshops, courses and keynotes, not to mention hundreds of virtual meetings. The first assessment I make is of the quality of attention in the room. How? Facial expression, of course, followed by body posture.

In July 2023, we were running a two-day program with banking graduates. There were close to 300 participants at the Sydney Convention Centre. After being introduced, I took the stage to start the program and immediately read the room. Anxiety was relatively high. Many faces had adopted neutral masks. Here and there, participants were fully engaged, engrossed in the experience, showing willingness to learn. One stood out. His facial expression conveyed deep, intelligent assessment. He was considering what he was hearing, determining its merit and value. He struck me as someone who had a stellar career ahead of him.

Here is the question: Is any of that true?

It was purely a perception I had, without any valid data to support it, based entirely on the quality of attention reflected in his facial expression.

What does this mean in communication terms? The answer is simple. Pay attention! In all your communication situations, decide to fully participate from the very beginning. A long-standing client told us once:

> *I love boring presentations and meetings, because that's where I practice full attention. If I can do it in those sessions, I can do it anywhere. Two benefits that have helped my career as a result are, firstly, I got noticed. When the presenter sees a room full of semi-comatose people, and one person fully engrossed, they notice you. Secondly, I'm being professional. I get paid to show up at my best. I have not been sleepwalking through my career.*

The highest form of respect you can pay another person is the gift of your full attention. It is driven by intention first, attention second and then showing this through your physiology.

On the Myers–Briggs Type Indicator, many of our facilitators, including Erica and myself, measure as introverts. We get our energy from within ourselves and tend to be more contained in communicating in normal situations. We have learnt to be more facially expressive because it benefits the audience.

Extroverts can sometimes be overly expressive. Put an extrovert and an introvert together in a boring meeting. Spot who is looking bored out of their gourds first. Managing others' perceptions of you is part of communicating effectively.

'Why can't you just be your authentic self? Why do we have to play these games?'

In response to this, we ask: 'What does authentic mean?' If you put the novice driver behind the wheel for their first driving lesson and say 'drive authentically', they would justifiably look at you as if you were bonkers. Musicians spend years mastering their instruments before they find their authentic expression. Actors can take decades before their authentic voice emerges. Why? Because they have been

DELIVERY

working on their craft, learning the skills and locking in the capability that will allow the authentic expression to flourish.

We operate from the premise that authenticity is found in intention. If your focus, your intent, is creating a positive, mutually beneficial outcome, that is authentic. It will be reflected in your eyes and your facial expression.

CHAPTER 14
AUDITORY

'The human voice is the most beautiful instrument of all, but it is the most difficult to play.'

Richard Strauss

For those of us who use our voices, it is fundamental to how we communicate. Our *voices* carry the *language* we use (see figure 14.1).

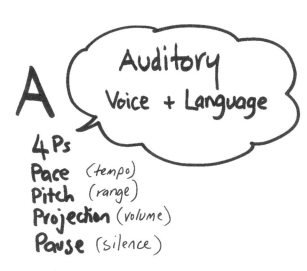

Figure 14.1: The auditory framework

Voice

The moment you hear someone's voice, you are making a bunch of assumptions and judgements. After you've spoken even one sentence, your audience has tracked some of the following, including your:

- emotional state (are you anxious, nervous, calm, confident?)

- background (culture, socioeconomic status)

- educational standard

- engagement (impressive, neutral, weak)

- intelligence

- sincerity

- authenticity

- trustworthiness

- conviction

- credibility

- likeability.

And that's just a few of the attributes.

Sadly, there are still hardwired prejudices linked to what you sound like, which can have implications for your life. It's not fair. It's not right. It just is. This is called linguistic profiling.

While accent modification is something people will choose to explore, in our work, we focus on making the best use of your natural voice. We call this *linguistic adaptability*. This is a skill that can be beneficial in all communication contexts. Adjusting your speech for clarity or mutual understanding without compromising your identity is a critical communication and influence strategy.

Have you ever heard your voice on tape or on video and been surprised at how you sound?

Most of us dislike hearing our recorded voices. We often hear people say that the recording doesn't sound like them. One of the reasons for this is bone conduction. When we speak, our voice reaches our ears through two different pathways. The first is through air conduction, which is sound transmitted through the air into our ear canal, which is how everyone else hears our voice.

The other way we hear is when soundwaves from our voice vibrate the bones of our skull and jaw, which directly stimulate the inner ear. This additional pathway enhances lower frequencies and gives our voice a fuller, more profound quality not present in a recording. Yes, your bones make your voice sound better to yourself.

'My voice has always been high pitched', a 22-year-old female graduate told us, 'and I think this causes people to take me less seriously.'

She is not wrong. High-pitched voices in work communication are often perceived as being less persuasive or lacking gravitas. Again, not fair. Just how it currently is. But, your voice is an instrument you can control. Like your posture and your gestures, you can learn to temper the different elements of your voice. We call them the 4 Ps:

1. Pace: the speed and tempo of your speech patterns

2. Pitch: the highs and lows, or range of your voice

3. Projection: volume, loud and soft, sometimes whispering

4. Pausing: allowing gaps and silence in your speech rhythms.

DELIVERY

We all have a natural way we use these four vocal elements. We all know people who speak fast; people who have loads of vocal variety; and, of course, those who are masters of the monotone.

Your voice is always a blend of the four elements working together. You don't play the piano effectively with one finger — unless you are Mr Bean at the opening of the London Olympics (look it up; it's hilarious).

Let's explore how each can be applied in your workplace comms.

Pace

The speed at which someone speaks can influence how the message is received. No surprises there.

We have heard many an executive say something like, 'Look, I only have ten minutes, and I've got a lot to get through', before proceeding at Formula One tempo, leaving their audience stunned and bewildered.

A moderate pace is the most effective for clear communication. Speaking too quickly can overwhelm listeners, making it difficult for them to absorb the information. Speaking too slowly can be perceived as disinterest or lack of confidence. What is needed is *variety.*

Have you ever watched a movie that feels 'one-paced'? Some critics might call it mesmerising, but for many, it just feels monotonous. A one-paced style of speaking or presenting reduces attention and becomes more challenging to follow.

I find overlong action scenes in movies, like car chases, tedious. There is one pace — frantic. We know the hero will live, so there is usually zero jeopardy. Variety in pace is critical.

The underlying principle with pace is to slow down. A slower (but not too slow) voice is perceived as more confident, more assured and more trustworthy. Imagine consulting with a doctor who speaks a million words per minute. It would be anxiety-inducing.

If you are naturally a fast talker, it will take conscious practice to slow down, but it's worth it to hold people's attention.

Slowing down your pace, your tempo, will enhance the clarity and effectiveness of your communication, especially in a work context. Here are some key strategies:

LISTEN

It might seem so obvious, yet few people do this. Start by becoming aware of your speaking speed. As mentioned earlier, recording your meetings or presentations and listening back will be an eye-opener. Awareness is the first step towards change.

THE POWER OF PAUSE

Use pauses strategically. We will go into this in depth on page 156. Pauses give you time to think and also give your audience time to absorb what you've said. The best advice I got on this was to think in beats, like in music. The beat before a chorus indicates a transition. Comedians are masters of the beat, because the timing of the punchline is as important as the words themselves. If I want to make a key point, I will have a pause, or beat, before making the statement. This immediately alters pace.

EMPHASISE

Slowing down when you emphasise important words will control your overall speed; for example, 'The next three weeks will be... *critical*... for the success of this project.'

BREATHE DEEP

Fast speech is a reflection of fast thinking. If you are anxious or nervous, your brain activity escalates. Breathe. Slow breath in, slow breath out. Practice mindfulness and techniques to calm your thought processes before the meeting or presentation.

Pitch

We all know that a monotone voice can be dull and disengaging, while a varied pitch can help to convey enthusiasm and keep the listener's attention. Just as a slower tempo adds gravitas, a lower pitch is associated with authority, and can be effective when you want to appear commanding and confident.

In our work, we have noted the importance of emphasis. We describe this as 'landing' on a key point, and this requires lowering the pitch on the key word.

'The most important attitude we can have to each and every customer is simple, it's ... *respect.*' The pause, or beat, before the word 'respect' sets up the audience. Following this by saying the word emphatically, in a lower tone, nails the message.

Once again, recording your voice will give you the feedback you need to build pitch awareness. Most of us are unaware of our default style. As you listen to the recording, consider how you could have said individual statements differently.

Time to work

Pick three paragraphs from a book to read aloud. Record yourself while you do this in three different ways.

First round: Use a conversational tone, as if you were chatting to friends.

Second round: Try a more formal tone, for example, as though you were in a board meeting. You are striving to be serious and thoughtful.

Third round: Imagine you are a motivational speaker — you are seeking to inspire.

As you listen back to the recordings, what do you notice about your pitch? Where did it naturally go up and go down? Practicing this will build your *pitch awareness* to add to your *pace awareness*.

I love listening to Edvard Grieg's Peer Gynt Suite No. 1, 'In the Hall of the Mountain King' to see how the power of pace and pitch combine to create an extraordinary auditory experience. Now imagine if the way you speak had that same effect? It will take work to find your voice and develop the conscious control necessary, and that's why you are reading this book.

Listen to powerful speakers throughout history. The cadence and rhythm of their delivery can almost be followed on a piano.

The soaring delivery by Martin Luther King Jr in his historic 'I have a dream' speech is still so powerful today. His emphasis on the word 'dream' became central to his message and contributed to how memorable it has become. He used pitch purposefully and powerfully to shape the thinking of millions of people across the world.

> *I have a* dream *that my four little children will one day live in a nation where they will not be judged by the color of their skin but by the content of their character. I have a* dream *today.*

Are there times when a similar passionate delivery style is appropriate in work contexts? We say yes. But only in the right context. When the outcome is to inspire, you have to sound inspirational.

DELIVERY

We have all seen people deliver powerful words without the powerful tonal value. An inspiring message delivered in a flat, monotone way will not inspire.

GOLDEN RULE WITH PITCH: STOP THE RISING INFLECTION HABIT!

One pitch habit to develop is ending sentences with a *downward* inflection. Some cultures, Australia most famously, have a vocal tendency to end sentences with a rising pitch. In the USA, it's called Valley Speak. The Kardashians have a lot to answer for.

The rising inflection, also known as 'uptalk' or 'high rising terminal', is a speech pattern where the pitch of the voice *increases* at the end of a sentence. This turns statements into questions. It's confusing. It also dramatically reduces authority.

In work-based communication, a rising inflection can convey a perception of uncertainty. If you are seeking to influence up the chain, to leadership teams and the like, your rising inflection will make your assertions sound weak, conveying uncertainty and reducing impact. Because a rising inflection may suggest a question or doubt, it will undermine authority and credibility.

As we explored earlier, listening to your recoded voice will give you the feedback you need. Because a rising inflection is unconscious, you may need to consciously practice. One of our participants, Belinda, developed a method to control her pitch by 'conducting' her voice by using her hand. She uses her hands to gesture, and the end of her sentences she would drop her hand to remind herself to lower her pitch. It worked for her. It could work for you.

Projection

Projection is about the *volume* of your voice. Speaking too softly can suggest insecurity or make it difficult for others to hear, while speaking too loudly can be perceived as aggressive.

Like pace and pitch, effective projection involves speaking with enough volume to be easily heard and understood without overpowering the listener. We have all worked with a shouter.

Projection is all about the experience and mood you want to convey. In our work, we will shift projection depending on where we are in our design. For example, in Step 2 (create relevance), we might consider a passionate tone, with a strong, authoritative projection. To support the relevance claims in our communications, we could include a story to serve as social proof. Here we would shift gears from strong projection to a quieter, more reflective tonality. The story shifts into a reflective state (and pitch), moving the audience on from the animating, louder tone of the relevance set up.

A passionate tone supported by a confident voice reinforces the relevance of your message. Increased projection adds power, connecting to your audience's heart and gut, but it does need to be supported by strong analytical and logical reasoning, which you will have worked on in your design work.

DELIVERY

Classical music is a perfect example of the control of sound. The quiet interlude, the booming crescendos, and the sweeping arcs of sound convey narrative and emotion. The conductor controls everything — pitch, pace, volume. You are the conductor of your music. The difference is your sheet music is words, not notes.

When we move to telling a story, we soften our tone and become quieter. If there is a reflective point being made, an overly loud voice will kill the chance for the listener to reflect on themselves. Storytelling also gives you a chance to apply the big gestures principle, in this case, big voice, as long it is congruent with the story.

If the energy in the group, around the table or in the room is flagging, a sudden change in sound immediately gauges attention. I occasionally shout as if I had a Eureka! moment when emphasising a point. 'Ahhhh! How about this!' said loudly immediately changes the energy in the room.

Pausing

A technology sales manager told us:

> *When I learnt the power of pausing, the way I communicated changed forever. In the past, I would be talking to the team and would firehose them with stuff, content and data. Now it is different.* **<pause>** *Now, what I do is this.* **<pause>** *I set up the point I want to make, and then…* **<pause>** *and then I make it! I don't overdo it, but when my team hear the pauses, they know something significant is about to be said.*

Pauses allow listeners time to process information, and they can be used to emphasise a point, create suspense or transition to a new topic. Persuasive, influential communicators are not afraid to pause.

And this highlights the challenge. In work contexts, people not only tend to talk too fast, but they also hardly pause for breath. There is this terror of the void. The silence. Perhaps they think if they speak without stopping, no one has the chance to interrupt them!

Anxiety and nerves also increase pace and limit pausing. The solution. Plan to pause.

People who read off teleprompters, like newsreaders, politicians and the like, will have directions on the teleprompter telling them to <pause>. I won't mention a business leader in Sydney, back in the 2000s, who, throughout his presentation, read the word <pause> out loud every time it showed up on his teleprompter. The experience was like a bad movie. The only thing people talked about after the event were his 'pause' references. No one could remember a word from the rest of his speech. His speech writer was horrified. His nickname immediately became Tiger — the cat with the big paws.

A starting practice technique is to think about pauses as you move through your design delivery. Once you have concluded the start strong, pause, then move into relevance. A pause can create expectations for the introduction of your concept. Before you move to managing FODs, another pause will signal the transition. In meetings, before you offer a point of view or a contribution to the discussion, use pauses like this:

> *I have two responses to what is being discussed.* **<pause>** *Firstly,* **<pause and anchor with a gesture to your right>** *I feel we have to be cautious. Going in to too soon could compromise our advantage.* **<pause>** *And, secondly...* **<pause and anchor with a gesture to your left>** *I am confident that we have the right people in place to grab the opportunity if we get our timing right.* **<pause>**

Read the above paragraph out loud, using the <pause> directions and notice how it sounds. It may feel a little contrived initially; however, this pattern of delivery will cause people to lean in and take notice. The combination of pauses and clean anchoring will make your message crystal clear.

PAUSES AND Q&A

This following technique will elevate your influence effectiveness instantly. Notice how often, when a person running a Q&A session gets asked a challenging question, they answer sharply, often with a slightly higher pitch. Result? They appear defensive. You will see this in political debates or when someone is being questioned on a news or current affairs TV panel.

This is where pausing becomes a superpower. Imagine someone challenges you in a meeting: 'That's not true! I've seen the numbers. It's much worse than what you're saying. C'mon. Get real here. Are you trying to hide something, or are you ignoring reality?' That statement is confrontational. Almost reflexively, you would get defensive. This is where the power of the pause comes in.

DELIVERY

Wait for two beats, take a slow breath and then respond. This break immediately asserts control. What you don't do is react! The person throwing the question at you is hoping you will react. Then they will have control. Your pause and breath re-establish your authority.

When we get to managing questions in Chapter 19, you will learn a host of Q&A techniques to demonstrate your control and mastery. The underlying principle of pausing is timing. However, variety in pausing is the key to managing control and demonstrating authority.

By applying the four Ps to your work communication, you will increase your effectiveness and your influence in a range of scenarios, such as meetings, negotiations and presentations.

Finally, is getting a personal voice coach worth the investment? In short, yes.

Some of us are naturally higher pitched than others. We have our fast talkers, slow talkers, people who are louder than others. A good vocal coach will guide you in using this most important instrument and fine tune your delivery for different work situations. While it can be difficult to learn a whole new way of talking, the payoff is extraordinary.

CHAPTER 15
LANGUAGE

Good morning, everyone. We need to make, what I call, a paradigm shift. The landscape has changed. We don't have greenfield options. Our ducks are not lined up in a row. To step up to the plate, we must be willing to play, and play hard. If we are all singing from the same hymn sheet, then we will succeed. The boat doesn't row itself, as we all know. At the end of the day, going forward, I know that every one of you, in your heart of hearts, knows how to put your shoulder to the wheel. We need to approach this strategically. We cannot let sleeping dogs lie. While we cannot boil the ocean, we must move the needle, so synergise, think outside the box, go after the low-hanging fruit and pivot to success. It's bootstrap time. We can climb this mountain. So, who is with me?

Have you heard this sort of nonsense before? Clichés and corporate speak abound in work communication. All workplaces will have their shorthand. We had a client conduct a global restructure and create a new department called something like Professional Services Delivery, which, naturally, was called PSD. Unfortunately, there was another global function called Product and Solutions Development, also referred to as PSD. Confusion reigned.

Acronyms, jargon, buzzwords and the like can and do come across as bland and dull. It's not that jargon is inherently bad. It is an efficient shorthand within specific groups who share the same context; however, it's important for leaders to be mindful of when and how it's used.

Plain language is the answer. 'Let's circle back and touch base about the key deliverables on this project next week' is something you might say at the end of a meeting. Jargon central. In plain language, the meaning of this sentence is, 'Let's meet next week to discuss the main tasks we need to complete for this project.'

'You are obviously committed to utilising best-of-breed solutions to enhance your customer-centric approach.' I use this example because I heard myself saying these words at a technology conference a few weeks ago. As they spilled from my mouth, I flushed with minor embarrassment.

What I meant to say was: 'You want the best available methods to improve your service for customers.'

Plain language takes work. We can get sloppy and rely on saying stuff that sounds profound but, on analysis, is just noise.

Reducing jargon

Have you sat in a meeting listening to someone and thought, 'I don't know what they are talking about ...' Listen carefully. Are they saying anything substantive? How much of their contribution is lost because of poor design or because it's littered with jargon and buzzwords?

Start with noticing how much conversation in business contexts is jargon exchange. Make it a habit to follow any jargon-laden sentences with a plain language explanation, especially when communicating with mixed groups where everyone may not understand the terminology.

Once you are aware, start 'listening' to yourself. How could you simplify your words? Senior executives deeply respect concise language. At the risk of using a cliché: 'Less is more'.

When using acronyms, check everyone understands what they mean. There have been several times when I've asked someone to explain an acronym and they simply don't know. 'I think it's the Central Procurement Department, of Centre of Procurement Deployment, something like that, we just call it CPD.' We, of course, think of CPD as the concept, principle, details in the CPD Hierarchy. Never presume.

Many years ago, I was facilitating a leadership team development program with Marvin Oka, who we talked about in Chapter 3. Our role was to help the team communicate more effectively. Simple. During our second session with the 12 participants, we were observing their interactions in a standard leadership team meeting. Marvin leant in at one point and said, 'Okay, you are going well. Please apply the Makins Method we learnt last week, and see how you go.' The group continued for a few minutes. Marvin stepped in again. 'Can anyone tell me what the Makins Method is?' Silence. No one knew because Marvin made it up.

The point Marvin was making was that we often pretend to understand what's going on because we are afraid that if we don't understand or don't know, we will be the only ones.

One of the benefits of diversity in teams is that language becomes simpler and plainer. With different language and cultural backgrounds in your workplace, it ensures that understanding is respectfully checked. Make this a habit in all your communication contexts.

DELIVERY

The scourge of '-ly' adverbs

'Has this investment delivered the results you wanted?'

'Absolutely!' is the response. The better answer is 'yes'. Why?

We use '-ly' adverbs to add emphasis. Compare these sentences:

> Let me **briefly** *say we were* **totally** *surprised by the results.* **Basically**, *we were expecting a better outcome. What we* **actually** *need to do is to* **fundamentally** *shift our approach because we are* **absolutely** *certain we have the right product. We* **clearly** *need to rethink our marketing strategy,* **obviously**.

Versus

> *These results are surprising. A better outcome was hoped for. This requires a shift in our approach because we have the right product. We will rethink our marketing strategy.*

Stripping out '-ly' adverbs is persuasive, clear and clean.

The unconscious effect of '-ly' adverb use is it reduces your impact. Let's take one example that is very common, the word 'actually'. The intention of the speaker is to bring emphasis and stress importance by chucking a bunch of 'actuallys' into the mix. The experience for the listener is the opposite.

'*What we are actually going to do is actually focus on what is actually important*', sounds desperate, pleading and lacking confidence. '*What we are going to do is focus on what is important.*' Simple, powerful, precise.

These '-ly' adverbs are unconscious fillers. You may not know how often they intrude into your work-based communications. Record yourself on Zoom or Teams calls and listen back to them. How often did you *actually* use 'actually'? What about the other unnecessary '-lys' that have snuck into your speech patterns?

Keep. It. Simple.

Fresh, zesty, surprising

When listening to someone articulate and expressive, it's impressive. Their vocabulary alone introduces unusual and evocative words.

Stephen Fry, the noted English author, intellectual and filmmaker, has a mellifluous tone in his beautifully crafted language application. His voice has entered the minds of millions of people, over one billion hours of audiobook narration, as his voice transports JK Rowling's *Harry Potter* books into three-dimensional imagined space.

I used the word *mellifluous*. Perhaps a word you rarely use. A joy of a word. It means pleasingly smooth and musical to hear. (I'm aware we just used a '-ly' adverb, but it was appropriate for the definition.) The joy of the word is its sound, which is also pleasingly smooth and musical to hear. It is autological as it sounds lovely.

You might be thinking, 'I don't want to sound like some poetic idiot at work', and we are not suggesting you do. The challenge is to expand your vocabulary to create a distinctive voice that lifts you above the everyday jargonistic drudge of standard work conversation.

Plain language

One tool that can help you simplify your language is artificial intelligence. Run your presentation through an AI program, such as ChatGPT, and ask it to turn the content into plain language.

Train your brain to simplify your ideas and contributions in meetings. Run the sentences through your own head, and then edit mentally before speaking.

On a virtual workshop during COVID, we were working with a US-based technology team. One of its members spoke in jargonese, which is now an actual word. Long, convoluted, corporate cliché–littered sentences were the order of the day. At one point, he said something like:

We need to align our constituent stakeholder ecosystem to maximise the potentialities and mitigate the risk factor variables, both known and unknown, in the realisation of the KPIs and OKR in our first and second horizon strategic intentions.

One of his colleagues, Sandra, had had enough. 'Phil, do you mean we need to ensure everyone understands and agrees to follow the six-month plan?'

'In essence, I concur, however, I thought it would be appropriate to ensure we had spotlighted the requirement', said Phil.

'In other words, "yes"?' said Sandra.

'Yes', said Phil.

That's plain language.

CHAPTER 16
VISUAL AIDS

We are so consumed by screens in our lives that we are always looking for visual support for what we are hearing. In a work context, your most powerful tools of influence are the words you say and how you use them. Adding visual support to your words, ideas and information *aids* the comprehension and understanding of your content, message or ideas.

In the last 25 years, it seems that visual communication has become the primary means of representing content. The role of the presenter now is to explain what people are looking at. This is not effective.

The most important visual aid is imagination. When your words create scenes, images and scenarios inside the heads of the people listening to you, you are connecting. You are genuinely communicating.

Showing stuff on a slide, and then adding some spoken words to their reading, changes the communication dynamic. As they read or look at the data, the charts or graphics, the audience will process the information they are reading first before tuning into what you are saying.

How often have you sat in a meeting where someone starts going through slides, then a question is asked about information on the slide that the presenter has not covered yet, and suddenly we are out where the buses don't go? The flow of logic is derailed, and at some point, the person operating the slides is forced to get people back on track. Time is wasted. The thread has to be picked up again, and then we are onto the next slide. The pattern then repeats.

Discussion, discourse and argument are how human beings have made sense of their worlds for centuries. The oral tradition still has a massive impact on cultural memetics. Words have power.

Shifting the locus of the focus from listening to reading/looking has changed how we consume information. In context, reading and looking is appropriate. You are reading right now. In work communication, where you seek to influence and persuade others, master the spoken word first, and then consider what visual aids will support your message or outcome.

Design first, completing the 12 steps, then consider what visual aids will support the outcome.

Most work communication design *starts* with visual aids. Big mistake. Why? Because you are now content-focused. Your attention is also on how the content is structured visually rather than considering the impact of the message, intent, meaning or emotional value because we are firmly in the grip of logic and analytical representation. Let's explore some other options.

Beyond PowerPoint

Before starting many of our training events, we often ask, 'Who here has been to a boring presentation?' A forest of hands goes up.

'Who has given one?' Laughter, with the same hands being raised.

When we ask the participants what contributes to boring, low-engaging presentations, slides are at the top of the list. Death by PowerPoint (see figure 16.1) is a standard description of poor use of visual aids.

FY24 Q4 Goals and key deliverables
FY24 Focus: Landing momentum, digital adoption, integrated performance reporting.

Priorities	Remediation	Momentum	Transformation
	⬡ Lorem ipsum dolor sit amet, consectetuer	⬡ Lorem ipsum dolor sit amet, consectetuer	⬡ Lorem ipsum dolor sit amet, consectetuer
Goals	① Lorem ipsum dolor sit amet, consectetuer adipiscing elit, ② Lorem ipsum dolor sit amet, consectetuer adipiscing elit,	① Lorem ipsum dolor sit amet, consectetuer adipiscing elit, ② Lorem ipsum dolor sit amet, consectetuer adipiscing elit,	① Lorem ipsum dolor sit amet, consectetuer adipiscing elit, ② Lorem ipsum dolor sit amet, consectetuer adipiscing elit,
Key deliverables	• Lorem ipsum dolor sit amet, consectetuer • Dolor sit amet, consectetuer adipiscing elit • Sed diam nonummy nibh euismod tincidunt ut laoreet dolore magna aliquam erat	• Lorem ipsum dolor sit amet, consectetuer • Dolor sit amet, consectetuer adipiscing elit • Sed diam nonummy nibh euismod tincidunt ut laoreet dolore magna aliquam erat	• Lorem ipsum dolor sit amet, consectetuer • Dolor sit amet, consectetuer adipiscing elit • Sed diam nonummy nibh euismod tincidunt ut laoreet dolore magna aliquam erat

Figure 16.1: Death by PowerPoint

We have all seen slides like these hundreds of times. Dense content. Difficult to read. Bland design. A classic death by PowerPoint format.

The content is essential. All the information on this slide is pertinent, relevant and necessary. The problem is *not* content-related.

Importantly, the content on the slide has the advantage of being structured as a CPD Hierarchy.

Concept: FY24 goals and deliverables

Principles: remediation, momentum, transformation

Details: two goals per principle and detail on deliverables.

DELIVERY

Good structure. From a content design perspective, we have ticked all the boxes. Now, it's time to deliver. This is where the problems start.

Mistake #1: Not setting up the slide

Most people will put up a slide like the one in figure 16.1 and discuss the information displayed.

Once a slide full of content is displayed, no surprises, people start *reading*. They endeavour to make sense of the stuff they are looking at. They will likely arrive at their conclusions without context, and we lay the foundations for misunderstandings. There is no frame of reference. If they are reading, they are not fully listening.

Framing the slide *before* it's shown is the key.

> *Let's understand the context before I show you the next slide. We are nearing the end of the first quarter of this year. We are doing well. Q1 will exceed expectations. Excellent work from everyone. 'What about Q2?' I hear everyone in the room asking. You are about to see the three priorities that will guide everything we do for the next three months. Here it is.* **<Click>**

Framing how your audience should digest the information, data or graphic you are about to display controls how people in the meeting will follow the logical path you are building.

Mistake #2: Showing the whole slide

Even if you have established a clear frame of reference for the slide, when a slide of such dense content is shown, people could still get confused or simply tune out.

What I'm about to say has been the source of fierce debate over the years. Time and time again, we have had pushback on this until the person tries it. It's this: animations are critical to ensuring understanding and, thereby, influence.

Start with the concept and use animations to build from there, following your designed talk track.

Let's look at the FY24, Q2 plan of action.

FY24 Q4 Goals and key deliverables

There are three priorities we need to lock into everyone's mind as we move into Q2. They are **<click>** *remediation, followed by* **<click>** *momentum, and finally, most importantly,* **<click>** *transformation.*

FY24 Q4 Goals and key deliverables

Priorities	Remediation	Momentum	Transformation

From there, you guide the audience's attention by revealing the content elements as needed. Who is in your audience, and the context, will determine the speed you go.

DELIVERY

FY24 Q4 Goals and key deliverables

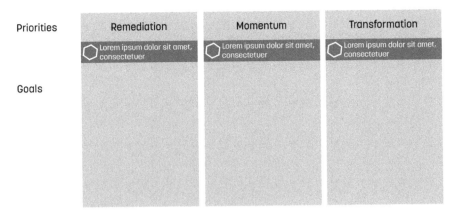

As you reveal the content, you add richness to the information, citing examples and reasons.

There are two goals for each priority. Easy to remember. Critical to achieve. Let's start with remediation. These goals are simple: fix and improve. **<click>** *Momentum will not surprise anyone: they are small business and customer engagement.* **<click>** *Now the exciting one — reshaping our business for AI. Two goals here: new propositions and getting the digital experience right.* **<click>**

FY24 Q4 Goals and key deliverables

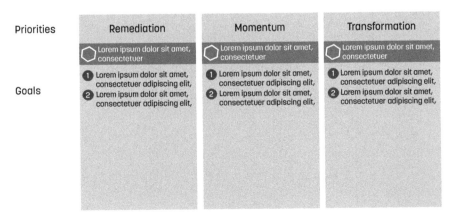

The objective here is a clean, smooth interaction between your verbal delivery and what is being shown on the screen.

'This will take forever!' is the response we often get. That is simply not true. Animation is similar to the good old-fashioned paper on an overhead projector slide. You only show what is relevant. This ensures alignment with the content. More importantly, you hold the attention of the audience. They cannot read ahead or come to their own conclusions. People often interrupt the speaker with a question about the detail in the bottom right corner while the concept is still being introduced.

We have encountered situations where the policy in internal meetings is no animations. The explanation is that it's frustrating to be controlled by the step-by-step process of revealing content, and it takes too much time. It's not the animations that are the problem. It's the delivery. The solution to this is ensuring a smooth alignment between words and revealing the next slide.

We watched a country manager deliver an astounding presentation at a kick-off event in Beijing. He had five priority areas to introduce to the 2000 people in the main auditorium of the Shangri La Hotel. A massive screen dominated the stage: one ground-to-ceiling screen that is now vogue for events worldwide (see figure 16.2).

DELIVERY

Figure 16.2: Huge screens are the current trend
Source: © Rawpixel.com/Adobe Stock

As he laid out his principles using anchoring, the words appeared behind him at the exact anchor point he was delivering from. It was seamless. More importantly, everyone in the audience was fully engaged. He built the plan on the slide; animation point by animation point.

Mistake #3: Too much content

How often have you heard someone in a meeting or presentation say, 'You probably won't be able to read this ...' as they click to the next slide. And there it is. Crammed content, tiny text, incomprehensible charts, micro bullet points. What is the point?

They then apologise, 'I'm sorry, I know there is a lot of content here.' As if there were nothing they could have done to fix this. We need to respect how people process information. The solution? *Chunking*

We covered the concept of chunking in Chapter 3, and the same principle applies to visual aids.

Slides with masses of content, information or graphics cause cognitive overload. We know that animations help with the cognitive capacity to absorb information on slides. That works. Or — and this will seem counterintuitive — have *more* slides. It's not the number of slides that matters, it's what's on the slides and how you interact with the audience or participants.

We know delivering content following a hierarchical structure, where smaller chunks are nested within larger ones, is effective. This hierarchical organisation makes it easier to understand complex information by breaking it down into interconnected chunks. Spread the content over several slides rather than packing everything onto one slide.

At a kick-off meeting in Singapore in 2012, the big boss says:

> *You are about to see three numbers. These numbers will drive everything we going to do this year. Everything. These numbers will be tattooed into your brain. All our work, meetings and everything we do must be headed towards the numbers we are about to see.*

The screen was dark. The anticipation in the room was palpable. The big boss reveals the first number. One slide. Nothing else.

> *This number is ambitious but doable.* **<click>** *This number will drive many of us to have the best earnings year ever.* **<click>** *And this final number? This will be a challenge. And we can achieve it. I know we can.*

One slide. One number. She could have easily had all three numbers on one slide, but spreading them out over three slides was much more impactful and engaging.

Chunking is closely related to language and memory. Language allows us to encode and communicate chunks of information effectively, and memory relies on chunking to store and retrieve information efficiently. Our words need to be chunked into CPD as well as the visual aids we use or create.

Pre-COVID, we had a client tearing his hair out because so many of the managers and leaders in the business simply did not know the company strategy. 'I communicated this to everyone', he lamented. 'I did a road show. Five cities in five days. It was exhausting. Almost every single employee attended the strategy sessions. I answered hundreds of questions. All the managers and leaders received the deck. What's the matter with these people?'

DELIVERY

I asked him to show me the PowerPoint deck he used during the roadshow events. He did — 120 slides, mostly packed with dense content, graphs, boxes, arrows, etc.

'How long was each session?' I asked. The state manager opened with a few words, introduced him as the CEO, he spoke for about 30 minutes before a 15-minute Q&A, and the state manager closed.

'One hundred-and-twenty slides? That's approximately one slide every 15 seconds. How did that work?' I asked.

'Of course, I didn't go into all the detail, but at least they could see how comprehensive this plan was. We paid a fortune to a consulting company to put this together. It's a great plan. The point is everyone got to see it.'

And there's the problem. He didn't *communicate* the strategy. He showed slides to people. Heavy, detailed content slides. In this case, the communication of the strategy failed. How do we know?

The meaning of your communication is the response you get.

The CEO blamed his managers, leaders and employees for not understanding the strategy *he* communicated. He did finally acknowledge that he was the cause of the confusion, and we fixed the problem. A visual aid aims to assist the understanding, meaning and comprehension of the information being communicated. There is a vast difference between the slides and the documents you provide. If I were going to explain an idea for a movie to a bunch of investors, I would paint a picture of the idea with words, describe the extraordinary characters, explain the appeal, and support this with some images and critical messages. Then I would hand out the script for them to read. What I wouldn't do is show each page of the script on a screen and ask the investors to read along with me. That's what most corporate communication looks like these days.

A good communicator intends to build and deepen interest. Only then would I provide documented validation for later reading and reference. If I used slides, they would be linked to relevance, concepts and principles, and finally, to the call to action. That's it. The detail is for documentation.

Remember, you design first, completing the 12 steps, then think about what visual aids would support the outcome.

Mistake #4: Slides on the whole time

On some of the remote clickers, there is the magical black screen button. Use it.

The moment nothing is projected on the screen, attention will turn to you. Our unconscious attention is drawn to light. If there is a screen on somewhere, we will look at it before looking at people.

How often have you been at a meeting or presentation, live or virtual, and the slide dominates attention even when the discussion or presentation deals with something entirely different?

One of the most straightforward techniques to control attention when presenting or using slides is to use the black screen option.

If you are presenting in an unfamiliar environment, make sure you arrive early to familiarise yourself with the tech. If you are operating your presentation from a laptop with PowerPoint slides, pressing the B key on the keyboard will trigger a black screen. Pressing the B key should get your presentation back (always test this beforehand as you never know when a software update will change the shortcut).

Virtual delivery is even easier. Stop sharing and go to camera view. When the slide is relevant, or you are moving to the next slide, go back to sharing mode. This dance between slide view and camera view is compelling, but it takes practice to make it smooth and seamless. The guide here is to ask whether the slide is serving the content or discussion? If not, go back to camera view. If there is detailed content on the slide, make sure people have time to read and absorb the data.

Controlling participants' attention in the meeting or presentation, both live or virtual, keeps them engaged and ensures everyone follows the content pathway you are laying down.

Mistake #5: Relying on the slides to remember your content

We have advocated against this lazy dependency on slides as your notes for years. A global technology leader sent us an email about two years ago.

Colin, after attending your course, I vowed never to rely on slides to help me remember my content. I worked hard on this. And then I got lazy. Lack of time was always my excuse. I was asked to deliver an update at an all hands town hall. There were about 200 people in the room and about 500 online. I had 12 slides. All good. I sent the deck to the organisers to incorporate into the master deck. I was confident that I could use the slides as my talk track. I didn't rehearse. The day came, the all hands kicked off. The GM started with the usual stuff. She then introduced me. I clicked the clicker, expecting my cover slide to come up. It was the wrong slide. I had sent the wrong deck. It was hugely embarrassing. After fumbling around for a couple of minutes, I realised I was not prepared, and I had to apologise and hand back to the GM. She stared at me. It was a brutal reminder of the lesson you taught us. Do not rely on your slides for content. You were so right. My GM was angry, but she has forgiven me. Never again.

Imagine an actor in a theatrical production of Hamlet walking onto the stage carrying a script. You would not be impressed. How about applying the same standard to yourself?

Think of it this way: if you are struggling to remember your content, how on earth will the participants at your meeting or presentation remember it?

Reading from prepared notes or a speech is acceptable only in certain circumstances. A critical speech, where the audience will dissect the words, such as a market analysis, means you have to follow the script to the letter. Reading is advised if it is a formal speech in a formal context, such as a eulogy. The emotion of the moment might take over, and having a well thought out, well-written eulogy ensures the speaker stays on track.

In this book, we focus on everyday work communication where laziness sees people follow the deck and extemporise around the displayed slide. You know someone is unprepared when a slide comes up, and they say something like, 'Oh, this one!'

If you need notes, all you need is a one-page outline of the 12 steps on your design, with a line or two against each step. A glance will keep you on track.

Mistake #6: Thinking you need slides

PowerPoint has become so ubiquitous we assume we should *always* have some slides in our meetings and presentations. Jeff Bezos, the founder of Amazon and a fairly wealthy guy, has banned PowerPoint slides in meetings. His argument is sound.

When new people come in ... they're a little taken aback sometimes because the typical meeting will start with a six-page, narratively structured memo, and we do study hall. For 30 minutes, we sit there silently together in the meeting and read, take notes in the margins, and then we discuss ... [20]

Makes sense.

Lewis D. Chaney, an American humourist, has meeting time worked out. He says:

In one year, in the United States alone, 19 044 YEARS worth of time in meetings (220 000 000 meetings annually x 45.5, the average meeting length, ÷ 525 600, amount of minutes in a year). [21]

PowerPoint slides create the illusion of work and thought at times. It's just too easy to whack a bunch of slides together, often copied and pasted from other decks, and then read them to a bunch of people who can already read.

Someone speaking eloquently on their subject, using the power of words, supported by PAVERS® methodology, following a clean design and logical structure is deeply impressive.

We saw this play out beautifully at a leadership team meeting in a bank two years ago. A new team member who had been in the role for only two weeks was talking about the risk function she had inherited. Let's call her Carol. She said, 'I hope you don't mind, but I'm not going to use PowerPoint slides', before proceeding with plain language, clean anchoring, and an authoritative vocal delivery to lay out her information for four minutes. When she finished, there was silence. Respectful silence. The big boss said, 'Thank you, Carol. I think you have challenged us all to lift our game regarding communication.'

That is influence. In four minutes, Carol had earned the full respect of her colleagues. The only reason you would ever use PowerPoint is because it *aids* understanding and supports the outcome. That's it.

Alternatives to PowerPoint

While we have treated PowerPoint as the generic term for projected information, there are other options for displaying content, data and information in meetings and presentations. They each offer different features, styles and formats that can help make your presentations more engaging and effective. Here are some popular alternatives.

Google Slides

Full disclosure: Google is a client of ours. Google Slides is a cloud-based presentation software that is free to use with a Google account. Google Slides offers collaboration features, easy sharing and the ability to work on presentations from any device with internet access.

Canva

Canva is an Australian company that has built some fabulous tools, including presentation ones. There is a huge range of templates, graphics and elements to create visually appealing presentations. Canva is user-friendly and great for non-designers.

DELIVERY

Prezi

Prezi has been around for a while and is known for its zoomable, nonlinear presentations. It allows you to create dynamic and visually engaging presentations different to the traditional slide-by-slide format. It's best used for storytelling and nonlinear information delivery, but it does take time to learn how to use it. If much of what you do is keynote-style deliveries, Prezi is a cool tool for creating visually engrossing presentations.

Keynote

Keynote is Apple's presentation software on Mac and iOS devices. It offers beautiful templates, animations and transitions. It's a great choice if you're in the Apple ecosystem.

***

There are a bunch more, and with emerging AI capabilities, the opportunity to create visually stunning presentations will become easier and easier, including movies, music and images that are all AI generated.

Warning: do not let form override substance. Remember, you are still communicating to *influence*. People might be entertained, bedazzled and amazed, but have you shifted them on the feel, think, do and commit to elements?

Remember, if your technology fails, you must still be able to deliver the outcome.

Flipcharts and whiteboards

We use flipcharts a lot. Our classic set-up in large venues is two flipcharts projected onto screens.

In smaller contexts, such as meeting rooms and the like, we find flipcharts to be an effective visual aid tool. And, of course, we have the same set-up in virtual delivery.

WHY FLIPCHARTS AND WHITEBOARDS?

As we know, PowerPoint is excellent for complex visualisations. Graphs, data, detailed timeline information and illustrations or graphic images are best delivered on a screen.

Creating handwritten diagrams and words in real time is highly engaging for the audience. As you draw or write, the audience can see the information taking shape before their eyes. This captures attention and makes the presentation more interactive and dynamic.

If you need to explain a process, workflow or even sophisticated concepts, the step-by-step creation of this makes it more compelling and memorable. But, it takes time! A slide can show something very quickly, even when building with animations; however, to physically create the visual aid in real time means the real-time construction aligns with the natural cognitive process of content or information.

You are also forced to keep it simple, ensuring the visual aid is just that, an aid to your delivery.

'My handwriting is terrible' is probably the most common objection we hear from participants. Our response is simple: learn to write

DELIVERY

neatly. Like any capability, it is a skill you can learn. My own handwriting is probably only legible to me. I use notebooks and a remarkable electronic notebook for client meetings or recording observations. My flipchart and whiteboard writing are very different. It takes practice. Alison, one of our long-standing facilitators, told me once, 'I think I practiced the content/method flipchart 50 times before I felt it was ready for the training room.' This is the discipline required to achieve excellence.

The other major benefit of using flipcharts and whiteboards is flexibility. You can adapt your content based on the dynamics of the meeting or presentation. If there are questions or discussions, you can incorporate them into the flipcharts, making the content more relevant and responsive to the room's needs.

We invariably get feedback like 'We *loved* the flipcharts. It made it more real. It felt personal. You were not waltzing in with a deck you have delivered 100 times before.'

Whenever we say to our participants, 'We don't use PowerPoint; is that okay?' you can see the relief on their faces. There is an authenticity and a more powerful connection between you and the audience.

Collaboration tools

Whiteboards and flipcharts have traditionally been used for brainstorming and workshops, such as design thinking. The problem is capturing all the good stuff, static whiteboards, post-it notes or sheets of flipchart paper, in both live and online meetings. Enter visual aid collaboration tools.

For both virtual and live meetings or workshops that need group work, like brainstorming, planning and discussions, many of these tools capture discussion and allow for collaboration. Here are some we recommend.

MIRO

Miro is a popular online whiteboard and collaboration platform that allows teams to visually capture ideas, create diagrams and collaborate in real time. There are loads of templates and tools for creating mind maps, flowcharts, diagrams and more. Teams work together on the same board, making it ideal for remote collaboration.

MURAL

MURAL is a digital workspace for visual collaboration. Like Miro, it has a variety of templates and tools for mapping out ideas, creating flowcharts and collaborating in real time. It's a brilliant tool for design thinking, brainstorming and agile planning.

TRELLO

Trello is a project management tool. We use Trello's boards and cards to organise conversations and tasks in our business visually. Its strength is creating visual workflows, tracking progress and collaborating with team members.

GOOGLE JAMBOARD

Google Jamboard is a digital whiteboard tool that integrates with the Google workspace. It allows for real-time collaboration, drawing and even adding sticky notes. It's suitable for teams using Google apps.

The best tool for you will depend on your specific needs, team preferences and the type of visual communication you want to achieve. Many of these tools offer free trials or basic plans, so you can explore them to see which one aligns best with your workplace and the work you do.

DELIVERY

Videos

The power of a short video to capture a message, share a customer perspective or provide proof of concept can be powerful.

The benefits of using video are many. They can capture the audience's attention and make presentations more engaging, especially when compared to a meeting full of slides. They also provide a visual element that can help convey complex ideas, data or concepts more effectively than words or static images alone.

The biggest benefit of videos is they are excellent for storytelling, allowing presenters to create narratives that resonate with the audience and help them better understand the content. And stories create emotional impact.

We saw videos brilliantly used at a manager conference in Dunedin, on the South Island of New Zealand, in 2022. The company was one of the largest producers and exporters of food in New Zealand and has a long and proud history. They live their values.

Instead of proclaiming the values, they showed short videos of employees sharing stories of how the values live across the organisation — from the farmers to transport staff, factory workers, IT specialists, quality control and sales. The videos were short. Powerful. Even now I can recall them. Some brought tears to your eyes. The framing of the videos by the MC was masterful. Superbly convincing. Deeply influential. It explained why their culture was so authentic and real.

Have you been to conferences where videos were used but simply were background? Too often these videos, which are expensive and time consuming to put together, are wasted.

At a Queensland customer event in 2023, I was sitting in the front row, waiting for the session to start. About 1200 attendees were filing in. The room got a little darker before a well-produced video started extolling the virtues of intelligent automation in hospitals using AI technology. It was slick. The narrator sounded professional. The story being told was powerful and convincing. A good video. Except for one thing. Half the participants in the vast conference room were still talking, staring at their devices or generally distracted. Why?

The video had not been set up.

When using video in conferences, meetings or presentations, it is critical, again, to *frame* what is about to be shown. In this case, all that was required was an MC or someone similar to settle the room and welcome the delegates before *framing* the video.

> *Welcome to this conference where we will explore the future of health care. Welcome. Are we all seated? Thank you. Thank you.* **<Allow the room to settle, and let the chatter quieten.>** *Welcome to the Future of Healthcare event, 2024. In a moment I'm going to ask you to put your phones away and focus on the screens. In the next three minutes, you will see why we are here, what is in store, and how you can contribute to this important event. Are you ready?* **<Show the video.>**

The amount of time, effort, energy and resources that go into video production is immense, so it's bewildering to us when we see these videos wasted so often.

Incorporating video can be highly effective when used judiciously and thoughtfully. We need to always balance the benefits of visual engagement and storytelling with potential technical and content-related challenges. Careful planning and consideration of the audience's needs and preferences are key to successfully integrating videos into presentations and meetings. The key is *framing* to guide attention, point towards value and support what follows.

There are videos you can use from YouTube, where no production costs are involved, but the principle remains the same. Frame first. Every time.

The downside of video usage is technical failure or disruption. 'We can't hear it. Turn up the volume!' Or there are bandwidth limitations. Tech checks are critical to this. Get to the meeting room early. Set up your stuff and check, double check and check again. The use of video needs to be seamless and elegantly incorporated into the meeting or presentation flow.

AI and the future

The tools in the AI world are expanding all the time and can assist you in designing, creating and producing visual aids. AI can make movies from just a few prompts. The entire movie production industry is under existential threat thanks to the power, speed and low costs involved in video and film production using the immense power of AI.

Jumping onto ChatGPT or an equivalent will take you to sites, tools and capabilities to assist you in creating incredible visual aids. Here is a warning: do not let form overtake substance. For example, ChatGPT can summarise your PowerPoint presentation just by you copying and pasting your PowerPoint content into ChatGPT and prompting it with, for example, 'Summarise the content from this PowerPoint presentation into 200 words.' Seconds later, you will have it. Microsoft, UiPath, Google and others have similar tools.

Explore. Create. And remember, any visuals you create are there to *aid* your communication; they are not the communication. Humans are still in control. For now.

Final thoughts on visual aids

To be a person of influence, it is still the power of your thinking, captured in good design and delivered with confidence, that will shift how people think, feel and behave.

Visual aids add richness, variety and engagement, but they are *not* critical. If the technology failed, your flipcharts combusted or your projector blew up, you should still be able to deliver the outcome.

DELIVERY

CHAPTER 17
ENERGY

As we explored earlier, we make a rapid judgement call when we meet people for the first time. This first impression assessment includes a bunch of things, including this rather intangible quality we call *energy* (see figure 17.1).

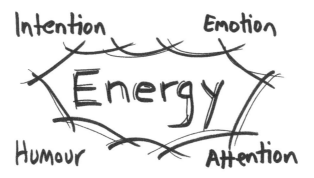

Figure 17.1: The energy framework

We convey energy all the time. In workplaces, this is often described as *attitude*. 'He has attitude, that one', someone might say of a colleague. In this case, it describes surliness, arrogance or conceit.

'She lights up a room when she walks into a meeting' is something you have heard. What do they mean by 'lights up'?

We have an array of descriptions for energy:

- upbeat
- docile
- sheepish
- alpha
- defensive
- moody
- petulant
- confident
- arrogant
- rock solid.

The list continues.

We continuously monitor energy to assess trustworthiness, integrity, intention, authenticity and motivation in every communication situation.

Some years ago, working with an extended leadership team, my role was to deliver a keynote presentation in the afternoon. I sat through the morning session, and the room felt toxic. Shifting eyes, masked expressions and wary postures were the order of the day. I knew why. People had lost confidence in the CEO. The energy in the room was a mix of mistrust and anger. The CEO said all the right words. People did the usual updates and the like, but the energy was off.

This intangible thing, energy, is felt in the gut and heart. A good communicator always reads 'the vibe' of the room and adjusts accordingly. Reading the energy of a room involves a mix of observation and intuition. We have all walked into a room where people have been arguing and can still feel the 'heat' in the room. Here are some key aspects to consider.

Start with body language

Observe how people are positioned. We have the easy stuff to observe, such as people having uncrossed arms, relaxed postures, looking comfortable, versus the classic closed body language with crossed arms, avoiding eye contact and people sitting or standing stiffly. What is important are the more subtle elements, such as tension in the shoulders or leaning or turning away from the speaker.

Micro cues in body language are subtle, often subconscious, physical responses that can reveal a person's true feelings or intentions. They can be fleeting and are usually more difficult to consciously control than larger, more obvious body movements.

A good place to start developing your skills in reading micro cues is facial expression. If you are in a relationship, you are doing this with your partner all the time. Have you ever seen your partner and immediately asked, 'What's the matter?' You are reading their body language, often at the micro cue level. A smile, frown or neutral expression can provide clues about people's mood and feelings. The face is incredibly expressive and can display numerous micro cues at once; for instance, a slight twitch of the mouth might indicate displeasure, or a quick raise of the eyebrows might show surprise or scepticism.

DELIVERY

Level of interaction

Notice how people are interacting with each other. Are they engaged in active conversation or do they seem isolated? The level of interaction can tell you a lot about the energy in the room. Is the energy polite? Is there an air of expectation? Can you gauge reluctance?

The volume of conversation can also be a good indicator. A lively room with lots of talking suggests high energy, whereas a quiet room might indicate low energy or concentration. Don't ignore your own reactions either. Sometimes your subconscious can pick up on cues that you're not consciously aware of.

Remember, these observations can vary greatly depending on the context and the cultural background of the individuals involved. It's also important not to jump to conclusions based on a single observation; look for patterns and consider multiple factors.

How energy affects the workplace

Hopefully, you have worked with or played in a team where the team spirit was incredible. The collective energy of the team was key to success, meeting obstacles or outperforming expectations. Interestingly, simply replacing a manager in a team can change the energy of a team overnight.

In our work, we consider energy the most important facet of effective influence. In the intricate dance of workplace interactions, the concept of energy often remains underappreciated yet critical in effective communication. The problem is how do you measure it? It's so subjective.

At its core, energy in the context of workplace communication is not just a metaphorical term but a tangible force that shapes and is shaped by every interaction, discussion and decision.

Think about the multifaceted role that energy plays in communication within the workplace. It affects team dynamics, individual performance and organisational culture. It affects your everyday experience. When you are feeling flat and uninspired, it takes conscious effort to get up and going.

When you communicate, you need to read the energy in the group, around the table or in the room. Energy serves as a barometer of engagement and morale. A team's communication often reflects their collective energy levels. When people are on automatic pilot, merely showing up because they have to, the energy can be dormant, neutral or flat.

Your job is to shift the energy. Find the energetic space to engage attention. We will learn how to do this on page 202.

Enthusiastic, positive energy can be infectious, leading to more dynamic and productive discussions. However, when someone is an energiser bunny, full of zip and sparkle, and not pacing the energy of the room, they can have the opposite effect.

DELIVERY

Managing energy

Energy management is tricky. Every organisation we work with talks about innovation. 'We must innovate. Innovation is fundamental to our survival.' Agreed. Yet, if there is no appetite for innovation, if people are exhausted by current demands, how do you find the energy for creativity and innovation?

Work environments that foster high energy levels are more open, encouraging vibrant communication channels where ideas flow freely and are received with an open mind. This energetic field encourages risk-taking and zesty thinking, idea bombs and tangential ideas — all essential components for innovation. On the other hand, a low-energy environment can lead to a communication climate where ideas are met with scepticism or indifference, stifling creativity and progress.

So, who determines the energy in a room, a group or even an organisation? It could be you.

As we have explored in the concepts of physiology and auditory, the role of energy in non-verbal communication is hugely important. Non-verbal cues like posture, gestures, movement, eye contact and tone of voice convey energy markers, bringing meaning to your words.

As a boat carves through water, it leaves a wake. What is the emotional or energetic wake you leave behind you as you go through the day? What is the energetic wake you leave behind having attended a meeting? Energy matters.

Source: © parkerspics/Adobe Stock

One of the most powerful presentations on this subject was delivered by the late great management guru Professor Sumantra Ghoshal.

Way back in 1995, Ghoshal was part of a panel answering questions at the World Economic Forum in Davos. He introduced the metaphor 'the smell of the place', contrasting the oppressive chaos of downtown Calcutta on a hot summer day versus the benign, cool embrace of the forests of Fontainebleau in spring.

> *Go to the forest in Fontainebleau with the firm desire to have a leisurely walk, and you simply can't... You want to jog or catch a branch or DO something... Most companies, particularly large companies, have created downtown Calcutta in summer inside themselves, and then they complain.*[22]

This is the energetic signature created by individuals, groups, teams and leaders in shaping the culture of any business, any organisation.

When the energy is open, if the 'smell of the place' feels invigorating, respectful and alive, employees feel empowered to express their thoughts and opinions, keeping the energy and communication dynamic flowing.

But a culture marked by fear, hierarchy and silos often leads to low energy levels, where communication is restricted and formal, lacking spontaneity and warmth, with the stink of anxiety in the air.

Energy is a vital element in workplace communication. It influences how messages are conveyed and received, shapes the dynamics of team interactions, sparks creativity and reflects the broader organisational culture.

DELIVERY

Using energy to influence

How does energy apply in delivery? Why is it within the PAVERS® framework? We will look at four aspects of energy:

1. Intention

2. Attention

3. Emotion

4. Humour

Intention

Let's come back to the principle: the meaning of your communication is the response that you get.

Very few people have the intention to upset or confuse others. In fact, in our experience, the vast majority of people are living their lives with positive intentions. Yes, there are those who are game players, manipulators and operating with nefarious intentions, but those people are in the minority. We need to be wary of them, but a healthy starting point in any human interaction is to assume positive intent.

Where there is a conflict or charged emotion, invariably it is poor communication dynamics at the root of the problem.

I recall travelling with a friend, Phillipa, many moons ago. She was driving in rush hour traffic in Sydney. We were talking away, and Phillipa was not fully concentrating. Bump! She nudged the car in front. It was very mild. This huge bloke threw open his door and came charging towards us. Road rage personified. Phillipa said to me, 'Watch this.' She immediately got out of the car and walked towards this bull of a man, hand extended: 'Hi, my name is Pip. I'm so sorry. You must be furious. My mistake. What's your name?' Smiling all the while. This 6-foot slab of anger took her hand, shook it and said, 'John, my name is John.' You could almost see the anger leave his body.

It was masterful. She diffused the situation in seconds.

Once the paperwork was handled (there was a tiny dent in the guy's car), I asked Phillipa how she did it. 'Intention. My intention was to support him by acknowledging he was upset, calm him down, solve the situation and move on. Simple.'

Not that simple. It took skill. How did she do this?

'I am so nervous before a presentation. I'm almost crippled by anxiety', is something we often hear. This can be solved by changing your intention.

If your intention is to make a good impression, to position yourself as credible, to ensure you don't stuff up or to demonstrate that you have done a good job, you might assume that these are *good* intentions to take into a conversation, meeting or presentation.

What's the problem? These intentions are in service of self. This is the foundation of self-consciousness. Most social anxiety, shyness or social awkwardness finds its origins in self-conscious intent.

DELIVERY

- Will they like me?

- Do I deserve to be here?

- Will they appreciate my work?

- Will I earn their respect?

- Will I fit in?

These are natural human concerns in any human communication context. We accept this and shift our focus to a more *constructive intent.*

Everything in communication at work is driven by a single focus — what is the outcome from the audience's perspective?

Constructive intent, therefore, is to focus fully on those who will be on the receiving end of your communication. Even if you are an attendee at a meeting, where you know you may have very little to verbally communicate, you can still bring the constructive intent of being present, listening carefully and supporting the energy in the room.

Flip the script. Rather than concerning yourself about whether they will accept or like you, have the intention of contributing from the start. Have the intention to give value and be a positive contributor. So often, at the start of programs, we will gauge the faces of participants, scanning for intent.

- Why are they here?

- Is there an energy of curiosity?

- Can we sense reluctance?

- Is there any anxiety or fear in play?

- Is there genuine excitement in the room?

This energy audit influences how we start the session.

In 2015, in front of an audience of 4000 very amped-up people, the energy in the room was out of control. It was Las Vegas after all. This was a huge event with famous people delivering sessions. I was the opening act: a four-hour workshop on leading in chaos. Lots of whooping, dancing (the music was loud), rampant excitement, through-the-roof expectations. The challenge the energy audit raised was how do we surf this without falling off. Suffice to say, it took a while to centre the crowd, to ready them for learning.

In any work situation, we can assume that there are multiple intentions in play. Some are playing politics, others don't care, some are hostile, many are neutral, there will be those wanting to play, wanting to contribute. The only real control you have is ensure you are operating from the cleanest intentions yourself.

With your audience in mind, your energetic intention is only this: how to be of service to the audience. That's it.

I remember going to an open-mic comedy night in Melbourne many years ago. It was an open-mic night where comedy wannabes had five minutes to make their mark. Tough crowd. Nothing more nerve wracking than having a few minutes to make an audience laugh. Many bombed. They were trying too hard. They wanted the audience to love them. Then one young guy came to the stage. You could feel his energy. He was not *taking* from the audience, he was *giving*. His name was Luke McGregor, and he is now a very successful Australian comedian, writer and actor. His energy was the key to how the audience warmed to him. No ego. No conceit. He is the only comedian I remember that night.

So what did Luke do differently? It was his *intention* and *attention*. Like all the other comedians, his intention was to make us laugh, that's a given; however, his attention was on us, the audience, not on himself. He was there in *service* of the audience. This instantly engaged everyone, and we reciprocated.

Can you spot someone who is self-conscious in a social situation? They look a little afraid, wide-eyed, rictus style grin. It's obvious. Their attention is on self—hence the expression. Someone who is socially relaxed has their attention on others.

If you feel exhausted after giving a substantial presentation, then you know you have done your job. When your intention is clean, when you are in service of the people in the room, you create the best conditions for a successful conversation, meeting, presentation or event.

This next idea might seem ridiculous, or even counterintuitive. The power of this idea, if applied cleanly, will have profound effects on everyone you communicate with. Your ability to influence will elevate exponentially.

One of most important ingredients for influence to occur, is when there is an environment of *respect.*

Respect is powerful. When people feel respected, they lift, they perform, they often outperform. Hopefully you have had the experience of a good teacher in your life. Your own Ms Knight. The number one consistent quality of effective educators is that they respect their students. Good coaches respect their players. Good leaders respect their teams. Good parents respect their children.

Here is the challenge. To be an excellent communicator, treat everyone you work with, communicate to or negotiate with *relentless respect.* Your default posture is respect. You start with the intention to fully respect whoever you are going to meet, whoever you are going to interact with.

This feels counterintuitive because in most cultures we are taught to do the opposite. People must *earn* your respect. Pause for a moment and reflect on this idea. When did your respect become so precious, in such a limited supply, that you parcel it out only to those who you deem worthy.

We all know the golden rule, treat others as you would be like to be treated, and respect is a solid foundation to start any relationship or interaction.

What immediately happens is you see people differently. Racism, sexism, ageism, any form discrimination operates from a starting position of disrespect. It has to. To vilify, condemn or denigrate others, even if you don't know them, has to emerge from a profound disrespect.

Layer on top of this, our socialised orientation to only respect those who are 'worthy', and you will notice how disrespect permeates though so many human dynamics. You can short circuit this and change communication quality quickly and effectively.

In our work, we see this all the time. At the start of a conference, an MC will welcome delegates and introduce the first speaker. We will see at least one-third of the audience still on their phones, sometimes talking, basically ignoring the MC.

This provides a significant opportunity for you to immediately stand out from others in any context you can think of, simply by having the *constructive intent* to treat people with *respect*. It seems absurdly simple, yet it takes conscious effort to reorient your perceptual filters, to train yourself to adopt this attitude and focus as natural, normal everyday behaviour.

This leads neatly to the next key to effective energy use, *attention*.

DELIVERY

Attention

The highest form of respect you can pay another human being is the gift of full attention.

Ask someone what their favourite childhood memories are, and invariably, they will tell a story about spending time with family, usually parents, where they were given their full, undivided attention.

In our distracted world, there seems to be a decline in our ability to pay attention. We are all bombarded with information via multiple channels, all day, every day. The devices, screens, billboards and websites are all fighting to grab your precious attention.

The emergence of the *attention economy*, a reference to the economic system where attention is considered a scarce resource, points to the battle to get your attention. Your precious attention. This is factored into business planning, go-to-market strategies and content creation.

We are all guilty of fractured attention, where we have a device in one hand, the TV on, while listening to a podcast and playing music in the house.

Industries are emerging where companies generate revenue by capturing and monetising users' attention. YouTube, TikTok, Instagram and other channels have seen the emergence of the 'influencer' phenomenon.

Attention matters. Your job as a communicator is to earn the right of your audience's attention. When there is full attention, the energy in the room or the meeting changes. You can *feel* the interest, the curiosity, the engagement.

STEP 1: PAY ATTENTION

Self-consciousness is misplaced attention. Having the *intention* to pay *attention* means your focus is external. This alone creates an energetic reciprocation effect. Because you pay attention to them, they pay attention to you.

In meetings, pay full attention. Listen to whoever is speaking with focused interest. Look at them. Create a metaphoric conduit of connection between you and the speaker. Your interest will be elevated, you will listen with more precision, and they will notice you. This is not your intent though, you are not doing this for gain, you do this because it enhances the quality of connection and communication.

STEP 2: READ THE ENERGY

As we explored on page 192, attention means you can gauge the mood or energy in the room accurately. If people are distracted, shut down or disengaged, it becomes immediately obvious, and you can adjust accordingly.

STEP 3: CREATE THE ENERGY

Your energy will be reflected in the people around you. Given the context and the outcome you are heading towards, what is the most appropriate energy approach? We have described situations where someone can say all the right words, but their energy kills or sublimates the message. 'We are in for a very exciting month', says a manager, with all the excitement of a shop mannequin. The disconnect between the words and the energy applied in the delivery mangles the message.

There are social situations where the 'energy expectation' is obvious. Funerals: sad and reflective. Weddings: happy and celebratory. Elevator: still and quiet. Football crowd: passionate and hopeful.

In work-based communication there is a bias towards neutral energy because it's safe.

DELIVERY

As a person of influence, consider the energy appropriate to the context. If it is announcing an innovative project, the appropriate energy would be excitement and heightened expectation. If the news is bad, for example, poor employee survey results, then the tone, or energy, needs to be more reflective and serious. The rule is alignment between message and energy to convey appropriate meaning — in other words: congruence.

STEP 4: CONGRUENCE

Your words must align with your energy, and vice versa. This leads to a fundamental principle: *energy is a choice.*

Have you noticed that you can 'turn on' energy as needed? This is something I see with parents. They may be tired and worn out, yet, when their child needs them, they find the energetic reserve to be there for the child. Fully there.

The metaphor most of us use for energy is the idea of a fuel tank. When your energy tank is full, no problem, you have energy on tap. As the day progresses, we have this notion of energy being used and running out. This metaphor makes sense; we are human beings who need rest to recuperate. However, a more useful metaphor for energy is something you plug into. Like an electrical socket.

In workplaces, you can see this when people around you look exhausted and downbeat — low on energy. Then it's time to go home. Suddenly there is this energy surge. Their bodies, attitude and vitality come to life. It's the 'happy Friday' phenomenon. When people plug into the weekend-coming-up socket.

What are your energetic choices? Are you constantly allowing the external world to affect your energy or are you in control? Are you taking responsibility for your energy in all contexts? Could you make better energetic choices in some situations?'

Taking control of your energy, being conscious of your energetic wake, takes practice and high self-awareness.

Online, in virtual meetings, demonstrate full attention by looking at the camera. We referenced this in Chapter 10. Looking down the camera and shrinking the meeting window on Teams, Google Meet or Zoom allows you to track reactions while you keep your eyes 80 per cent of the time on the camera. People feel seen, they feel your attention, and the energetic engagement follows.

Emotion

In written communication, usually texts, WhatsApp and other social media platforms, the liberal use of emojis supports the emotional tone of the message. It becomes a shorthand way of demonstrating intention and emotional meaning. The emojis do the emotional heavy lifting.

On virtual calls the emoji button can signal responses, approval, acknowledgements and the like. These are graphical expressions of emotions to support the meaning.

In live, face-to-face interactions, we cannot whip out an emoji card, we need to rely on bringing the right emotional resonance to the delivery.

As we explored in Chapter 14, your voice does a lot of work in ensuring you convey the emotion appropriate to the message and outcome. We also need to add the energetic resonance to support the words you say, the tone of voice, the gestural and postural elements to ensure your message is *felt* as well as understood.

DELIVERY

Of course, your words are important. That's a given. But it's the tone and emotion behind the words that truly matter. Effective communication is felt. Meaning is a full body experience.

Joseph LeDoux, the noted neuroscientist and author of *The emotional brain*, says: 'Emotion is the fast lane to the brain.'[23] His research on the neural mechanisms of emotion and the brain's role in processing information, confirms how important emotions are in effective communication.

If you don't feel you can trust someone, you are unlikely to be influenced by them. Probably the opposite. You would discount anything they might say.

Politicians manipulate emotions, particularly fear, anxiety and anger, to progress their agenda. The content, or facts, may be completely untrue, but the emotion is what carries the day.

Emotion matters. How do you bring emotion into your communication effectively?

STEP 1: FEEL IT

Authentic energy is felt. When someone is passionate about their subject, it's compelling. If they are angered by injustice, it's powerful. When they are moved and genuinely touched by something, it's real.

Using the idea that 'energy is a choice' will take time, practice and focus to let go of anxiety or self-consciousness and find the emotional value of the words you are saying to connect with your audience.

This is not easy. We are so schooled into work mode, where there is a robotic vibe in how business is conducted, where showing emotion is perceived by some as a weakness, that to step over the safety fence of neutral expression seems, to some, a step too far.

We are not advocating that you stand in front of your work colleagues and weep. Emotion is an energy that has to be considered and applied for one reason and one reason only: it serves the audience and the outcome.

Find that emotional space and let that be experienced in your words, in your voice and in your actions.

STEP 2: ACKNOWLEDGE IT

There is a lot of shit going down in business, governments, organisations and groups across the world. Anxiety is high. Uncertainty is everywhere. Every organisation we work with seems to be going through a restructure, a downsize, a re-size (whatever that is) and constant, relentless change.

Acknowledging what people are feeling, recognising their emotional state, is respectful, builds rapport and aligns the energetic field in the room. In Chapter 4, managing FODs dealt with the emotions linked to the audience's fears, objections and doubts. Denying or ignoring FODs will derail your communication.

In 2017, we were working with a middle management group of a large insurance firm. The mood in the room was edgy, almost hostile. We were not expecting this. Our diagnosis revealed that this group of managers was interested in their development, and the quality of the pre-work supplied demonstrated commitment. It was strange.

Alison, the facilitator for the program, delivered a powerful start strong, had a super tight relevance case, introduced the concept before attempting FOD management, but the mood in the room did not shift. Glum stares were the order of the day.

Alison finally stepped to the side of the room and asked: 'What is going on? You all look angry and pissed off. Your pre-work was

DELIVERY

excellent. Every indicator in our prep showed you wanted this, but now we have a room full of disgruntled people. I don't know what to do. Do we stop now and call it a day? Can someone tell me what's going on?'

Silence.

Alison waited. She held the space. Did not move. Eventually one of the participants said, 'The issue is not you, Alison. We were all looking forward to this. The problem is the three people at the back of the room, the HR observers.'

On a previous program, these same three HR folk had done the observing thing, then had written comments in reports about the participants that were based on their opinions. This had angered everyone. Challenging conversations followed. There was rancour in the air. The group had no trust in the HR people, hence their sullenness.

'Easy fix', said Alison, and asked the HR people to leave. They did so with muttering reluctance. The energy in the room changed instantly. 'They all cheered, as if released from captivity. It was amazing. I simply started again and the program was a huge success.'

If Alison had ploughed on, the day would have been a failure of effort and a waste of time. Acknowledging the energy was critical to the outcome.

STEP 3: DIRECT IT

Direct the emotional dynamics in the room. We return to a well-covered principle: variety is key.

Imagine a movie that is just action, action, action. The emotion is at adrenaline junkie levels for two hours. I know I have already mentioned that I find that to be insufferably tedious.

As emotion is always in play, read the energy to know when there is a need for respite. If the conversation has been bogged down in energy-sapping detail, find a way to lighten up, to relieve the tension. It could be as simple as a quick stretch break. Much like a conductor manages the orchestra, you manage the emotional ebb and flow of the conversation. One of the most potent tools to use here is stories, which we will be digging into soon.

This leads to our final element of energy management: laughter.

Humour

The sweet relief of laughter. It is an excellent regulator of energy. When people are feeling flat or disinterested, laughter immediately pulls them into the present and an injection of energy occurs. Humour jolts the body in reaction.

Humour serves several important social and psychological functions, while shifting energy dynamics in communication settings. Like most people, when you watch comedy shows, you may chuckle, but you probably rarely laugh out loud. We laugh aloud with others as a form of social bonding. Laughter unites. When we laugh together, we have a shared experience and camaraderie ensues. This social aspect of laughter is crucial for building and maintaining relationships.

We *need* to laugh. In workplaces this does not mean, clutch your belly, fall down laughing; it can be muted chuckling. The point is, we need humour in workplace communication.

Why?

Humour triggers the release of endorphins, the body's natural feel-good chemicals. It reduces stress and promotes a sense of wellbeing. In some situations, this is important, particularly when there is a need to alleviate tension and anxiety.

As always, we must be careful. Sometimes tension and anxiety are necessary. If we are dealing with a difficult and stressful situation that requires focused attention, laughter can distract us from the work at hand.

'I'm not funny. I'm not a comedian', might be something you are thinking. And, you are right. This is not about telling jokes or stand-up routines, it's to do with energy. Try simply shifting your energy to a lighter tone, smiling and saying: 'Okay, let's all take a deep breath. Phew. I was forgetting to breathe for a moment.' This is humour. It changes the temperament, interrupts the pattern, changes the pace.

Humour creates energy, but it's a double-edged sword. One side can cut the tension, but the other can wound and offend. Using humour to manage energy in a room needs to be done carefully with full awareness, and the risk of offending, no matter how mild the joke might seem, is high.

In one meeting, to illustrate the problem with silos in the organisation, one of the participants asked, 'What do a vulture and a brick wall have in common?' Others in the meeting looked at him, waiting for his answer. 'They both can't drive a car.' I thought it was quite a clever little joke — the only thing in common is what they don't do. Innocuous. Until one of the participants said: 'Are you mocking me because you know I don't drive?' The meeting was distracted while this was sorted out.

Political correctness needs to be considered. Whatever your position on it, care has to be taken that your use of humour does not distract from your goal.

CHAPTER 18
RELATIONSHIPS

Every social and communication situation is about the relationship created in the context. Something as simple as catching an elevator has lots of social rules and relationship dynamics. In a crowded elevator we know that we adopt a neutral attitude and posture, all face in the same direction, stand equidistant from each other, stay quiet. These rules are understood. They ensure we will be safe and indicate we have all agreed to travel together in this small box with minimal interference.

These social rules are learnt through experience. In workplaces, the relationship dynamics are a lot more complex. To influence effectively, your need to manage the relationship dynamics in the conversation, meeting or presentation.

The PAVE elements (physiology, auditory, visual aids and energy) are all employed here (see figure 18.1, overleaf). We will look at five elements, going into loads of detail on the last element, managing questions. The five relationship skills are:

1. Using names

2. Maintaining eye contact

3. Respect

4. Using questions

5. Managing questions.

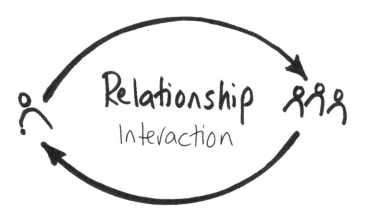

Using names: research audience backgrounds
Maintaing eye contact: show interest and sincerity
Respect: communicate as an equal
Using questions: rehetorial and direct
Managing questions: design in the moment

Figure 18.1: The relationship framework

Using names

Dale Carnegie in his brilliantly titled book *How to Win Friends and Influence People*[24] promoted the idea of always using people's names. People appreciate it when you remember their name and use it in conversation. As Dale Carnegie said, 'A person's name is, to that person, the sweetest sound in any language.'

We spend hours preparing for our programs, including reading up on every delegate or participant, and endeavouring to memorise their names, where they are from and what they do. It's a lot of work, and it pays big dividends.

The simple acknowledgement of someone, referencing something about their role, or a recent data point associated with their work, is profound. Feedback from one London-based participant came via her manager. In our research, via her LinkedIn posts, we discovered that she had been nominated for a Women in Technology award. This was mentioned during the program by our facilitator and she was stunned. In her email to her manager she wrote,

> *... not only did the facilitator and the coaches know everyone's names, their roles, how long we had each been with the company, but they had found out about my award nomination. I had been reluctant to tell anyone, but the facilitator acknowledged it and I have been flooded with support. I've never experienced this level of deep respect in a training program before.*

Let's acknowledge the reality of the busyness of most of our lives. To spend time and effort to research people who will be in your meetings, learning their names in advance, an interesting data point about them, and so on is an effort. Is it really worth it? Test it and see for yourself.

Reflect on your own career. Was there a time when a senior manager passed by and greeted you by name? I hope so. That is a sweet moment. And, no surprises, your respect and regard for that manager took the lift to the top floor of your list of leaders you admire. Instantly. Just because they knew your name. This demonstrates care. It demonstrates respect.

Many people believe that they are terrible at remembering names. It's important to set up a clear intention to remember people's names. This will change your attention and focus, which results in an increased ability to remember and recall the information.

DELIVERY

Whenever you are introduced to someone, ensure you not only say their name, but that you say it correctly. In our multicultural workplaces you might encounter unfamiliar names. Check with them that your pronunciation is correct. This simple step demonstrates that you are not performing the unconscious rituals of hello, goodbye and forget. You demonstrate care and full attention.

Maintain eye contact

The elements in human interaction (physiology, auditory and energy) play a role in conveying information, provide meaning and support the message. Eye contact plays a significant role in workplace communication and can have various effects on interpersonal interactions.

Imagine you are sitting in a face-to-face meeting and someone makes a contentious comment, borderline offensive. Watch people's eyes. Everyone scans the room, looking for an ally, and the eyes do all the work. 'What is he doing?' 'Uh oh, this could be trouble.' 'This could be a career limiting moment!'

Maintaining appropriate eye contact establishes trust and rapport between individuals. It conveys sincerity and attentiveness, making the speaker feel heard and valued. Simple, but true. We talked about the power of attention in Chapter 17.

In effective communication, showing interest, engagement and understanding in a conversation sets up the best conditions to influence.

We have all had that awkward experience of talking to someone at a work event while they look over your shoulder or simply look away. It's uncomfortable. *Lack of eye contact* or excessive avoidance is easily interpreted as disinterest or discomfort, making you feel uncomfortable.

Maintaining eye contact indicates you are focused on the conversation and the person speaking. It enhances the perception of the speaker's credibility and the seriousness of the discussion.

It goes without saying that you don't stare with an unblinking gaze. That's just creepy. Or intimidating. The objective is the gaze of respectful attention.

Remember the intention and attention elements of energy from Chapter 17. Eye contact conveys an incredible range of emotions, including empathy, sympathy, anger or frustration. The ability to read these emotional cues through eye contact is an essential aspect of workplace communication. Threat, humour, sincerity, disinterest, contempt, trust, love, hate, fear, anxiety, confidence, joy, playfulness, compassion, wonder, amazement, shock, calmness, happiness can all be expressed through the eyes alone.

We are unconsciously assessing every social and work environment with our eyes. We take in a range of social cues, relationship dynamics, rules, threats, situational guidance in seconds. This informs us of the role we play or how we will choose to engage.

As a master communicator, you can influence those around you simply through eye contact. For example, in group discussions or meetings, eye contact can be used to signal who should speak next or who has the floor. It helps in managing the flow of conversation and prevents interruptions. An eyebrow raise indicates to someone that they will be heard in a moment. A slight frown could advise them that it would not be wise to say anything right now.

In your next live meeting, track people's eyes. Become hyper-aware of how much work their eyes are doing in the meeting flow. If you have children, you know you can manage them with 'a look'. 'That's enough now!' 'Well done, you're a star.' 'What do you think you are doing?' These can all be conveyed with a conscious glance.

DELIVERY

We won't go into depth here, other than to say it's important to know that the role and interpretation of eye contact does vary across different cultures. In some cultures, prolonged eye contact may be seen as confrontational, while in others, it may be a sign of attentiveness and respect. Do your research on this. In some European cultures, overuse of eye contact creates discomfort or conveys disrespect so, again, we circle back to intention. Your eyes will signal intention more clearly that your words.

'What about virtual meetings?' Virtual meetings do not allow for all the intimacies and subtle social cues we convey when we are in the same room. Looking at the camera was discussed on page 101, but the down side of this is you miss out on nuanced non-verbal communication. It's difficult to get around this, as the benefits of maintaining virtual eye contact through the camera is more important than looking at the actual faces on your screen. The good old 80:20 rule applies here: 80 per cent of your time is spent looking down the camera; 20 per cent tracking audience engagement and responses.

Conscious use of your eyes becomes a powerful tool to connect, convey intent and facilitate communication flow. Ultimately, your goal is to show relentless respect.

Reset your respect

On a hot afternoon in Sydney in 2012, I was walking from a carpark to a meeting in Sussex St. From a distance I could see someone squatting on the pavement, a half a bottle of vodka next to them. As I got closer, I could see the drunken desperation on this young woman's face. Here she was, drunk on a city street, vulnerable, alone, yet everyone blanked her as they walked past, getting on with their own busy, busy lives.

I was wondering what to do, when the woman in front of me slowed, and I could hear her saying, 'Have we got ourselves in a place we don't want to be? What's your name love? I'm Maria.' She stopped in front of the woman. 'Leave me alone', the drunk woman spat. Maria responded with, 'Of course I will. Let's just have a quick chat first.' She sat down on the pavement next to the woman.

'Can I help?' I asked Maria. 'Thank you, we are all good. Just going to have a chat with my new friend here.' I walked on, crossed the road and stood watching from 40 metres down the street. Maria was talking, at one stage placing her arm around the shoulders of the now weeping woman. Five minutes later an ambulance arrived.

This story exemplifies *respect*. Maria saw a person in need. She did not condemn her, label her a drunken homeless person or simply ignore her. Maria did something, for a stranger, that may have been a defining moment in that young woman's life.

We have discussed respect before. It is one of the most powerful energies in human interaction imaginable. We see the flipside of this when people feel disrespected, they often react with anger or even open hostility and aggression.

To reiterate a message we already know, attend every communication context with full respect.

I include this story to demonstrate unconditional care and respect for someone in a desperate situation. Maria is a hero. Full stop.

How do you think of people you work with?

Let's be honest, we all have a mental filing system. Who in your life have you placed, possibly on very limited information, into the 'loser' file or 'idiot' file? Have you placed some people in the 'keep happy because they have power' file? The best communicators are more tolerant and open to others. Instead of reducing people to simplistic labels, we see their complexity. We respect that, just like all of us,

DELIVERY

they have their anxieties, guilt, shame and doubts. Like all of us, they have their blind spots and lack of self-awareness.

Respect is an act of generosity. Empty the filing cabinet. Reduce the instinct to label. Appreciate the complexity of every human being. Make respect your default position. The effect this will have on others will be profound and elevate your communication effectiveness dramatically.

Using questions

Questions are very effective in facilitating interaction, both tactically and strategically. Questions are used as a way of maintaining a sense of dialogue in the meeting or presentation, even if there is no direct response.

We are talking about two ways of using questions: direct and rhetorical.

Incorporating a mix of direct and rhetorical questions will make meetings and presentations more dynamic and interactive. The key is to use them strategically: direct questions for engagement and clarification; rhetorical questions for emphasis and thought stimulation. The goal is not just to ask questions but to *listen actively* to the responses, using them to guide the meeting effectively.

Direct questions

Have you noticed how often questions are posed in this book? They are designed to stimulate your imagination, reflect on your experience or to consider the future.

Engagement questions are used to engage specific individuals or the group as a whole. Their purpose is to clarify points, ensuring that everyone has a shared understanding of the topic or issue under discussion. These types of questions allow you to assess the understanding in the room.

Does that make sense?

John, I can see how this will be of most interest to you. Does this clarify the situation?

Are we all clear on the task at hand?

How many of you have come across this problem in your area?

Maria, I know this has been an obstacle until now, can we work on removing these barriers?

Has this been discussed in your teams?

Has this been bothering you?

The nature of this list of questions is to elicit nods or, occasionally, some commentary. Be careful to read the energy. People can sometimes nod or agree to disguise their confusion or resistance. If in doubt, double check.

Direct participation questions are looking for answers or a response. These can be used to get input from quieter members, giving them a platform to share their thoughts. They also can nullify opposition or give the floor to those who may be in opposition. In this case, you control their input versus being interrupted.

Mark, you know this better than anyone in the room. Can you share some of your thoughts on the first line risks from a customer perspective?

Andrea, we have discussed this before, and I know you have concerns. Can you expand on what you have just heard?

DELIVERY

Xiang, the marketing project is getting near its end. What have been the wins you and your team have achieved?

Rupal, can you provide the group some additional insight into managing this challenge?

I know we can't see you Joan, your camera is off, but your views on this will be valuable to everyone. Can you talk a little about the Johnson & Johnson account?

Using this approach early in the meeting or presentation keeps people on their toes. They better listen. Once they know you could call on them at any given moment, they move from observer to participant in a heartbeat.

Participation questions also encourage different viewpoints on a topic, enriching the discussion and potentially uncovering new insights. One FOD often in play is that everyone is supposed to passively follow the party line. Your encouragement of diversity of thought is respectful and demonstrates your confidence in managing the dynamics in the room.

Techniques for effective use of direct questions requires three elements:

1. Be specific: Tailor your questions to the individual's expertise or to the group's knowledge level. If your question is too generic, vague or ambiguous, your response will be silence.

2. Balanced participation: Ensure that you distribute questions fairly, avoiding over-reliance on the noisy, confident voices. When you ask a question of a quieter person, ensure you acknowledge their contribution thoughtfully and respectfully. 'Thank you, Lisa. This is exactly what we all need to be aware of. Thanks for bringing light to this. I had forgotten to do so — excellent.'

3. Follow up when required: Use these questions to delve deeper into responses, show active listening and encourage further participation. Be careful not to get too diverted or too specific. Stay within the boundaries of your CPD plan.

Rhetorical questions

As you know, a rhetorical question does not look for an answer, but is used to emphasise a point or to create a persuasive effect. The main characteristic of rhetorical questions is that the answer is usually obvious and understood by both the speaker and the audience.

Let's say you want to emphasise a point and encourage people to reflect on the issue in relation to climate change. You might say: 'Isn't it obvious that we need to act now to protect the environment?'

The difference between this idea being posed as a rhetorical question versus making a statement, such as 'We need to act now to protect the environment', is that the question implies agreement. Adding the word 'obvious' implies it's irrefutable.

If you want to criticise or point out a problem, you might try: 'How long can we really expect our customers to put up with our shoddy service in our call centres?'

You can use questions to introduce drama for emphasis: 'Aren't we all sick and tired of the bullshit politics going on between our departments?'

Questions can assist in the transition to a new topic or to the next principle: 'Okay, who has been waiting for this one? The role AI will play? Have we all been wondering how this will affect us in our day-to-day operations? And how this is going to relieve us of hundreds of hours of tedious admin?' The rhetorical question here doubles up as a simple and elegant frame for the next step in the conversation.

They can also be an effective tool to challenge or provoke: 'Have we really thought this through? Could we be making a big mistake here?'

Finally, use rhetorical questions to encourage reflection, giving pause for thought: 'What would happen if we simply did nothing? What if we don't react but simply ignore it?'

In each of these examples, the rhetorical question goes beyond simply seeking information. It's a tool for persuasion, reflection or emphasis, making it a powerful element in speech and writing. Techniques for effective use of rhetorical questions requires two elements:

1. Timing: Use rhetorical questions at pivotal moments to highlight transitions or important insights. Overuse of rhetorical questions can become tedious and predictable, for example, 'Would I be right in saying that you all agree?'

2. Tone and delivery: It's all about the tone. So often we have seen people ask a direct question, expecting an answer, but the tone implied it was rhetorical. This is followed by an awkward silence. If you do have a direct question, you can frame it by saying, 'I would like your thoughts in response to this question.' This ensures there is no doubt.

Using questions creates the experience of participation and engagement. People in your meeting or presentation will feel they are engaging with you rather than just listening to you.

The fifth skill is a core skill in managing the relationship element of PAVERS®, and is fundamental to being a person who can influence anyone, anywhere, every time. It's so central to your skill set that it warrants a chapter of its own. We will come back to the final element — Story — after we have gone deep into the art and skill of managing questions.

CHAPTER 19
MANAGING QUESTIONS

We can conduct an excellent diagnosis.

We can put together a superb 12-step design.

We can incorporate all the PAVERS® elements into the delivery.

Then comes the Q&A.

This is the test of your content, your credibility and your ability to manage dynamics in the room that will lead to influence.

Input, throughput, output

Using the systems theory as our starting point, we acknowledge that all communication follows an input, throughput, output flow in every communication context.

Inputs are the resources, information, participants and preparation that go into a meeting or presentation before it begins. Your diagnoses and design work is part of the input for the session.

Throughput refers to the processes and interactions that occur during the meeting or presentation. This would be the content, or the words, of the presentation or conversation, supported by any visual aids, discussion, workshops or other processing aspects of the session.

And, no surprises, the *outputs* are the results, decisions, actions and knowledge gained from the meeting or presentation and the questions that arise from the throughput phase.

If you leave a meeting or presentation with more questions than you went in with, the output phase has fallen short.

The Q&A phase of any communication scenario allows for clarification of points made during the session, ensuring that the audience has a clear understanding of the material, data or content. It's also an opportunity to elaborate more, with stories or use cases; bring the content to greater relevance and value; and importantly, to address concerns that may arise.

But, if you are unprepared, get defensive, over-answer (all too common) or misread the questions, you can be in a world of pain. Q&A is critical in the influence process. You have to master this.

Managing questions in three steps

The speaker finishes strongly, glances at their watch and says, 'We have 15 minutes for questions. Are there any questions from anyone?'

Invariably there is an uncomfortable pause. Who will ask first? If there is a high-status person in the room, there will be an expectation that they might ask something or make a comment. Or there is the extrovert who always, always asks a question regardless of merit or substance.

Once the question is asked the speaker will invariably address their answer to the person who asked the question. They will reiterate or clarify what people have already heard, and the energy and quality of the attention in the room drops.

Managing questions requires a bunch of skills:

- knowing how to read the motivation of the question

- diagnosing what type of question is being asked

- being able to formulate or design a response in real time

- answering in a confident and convincing manner

- keeping the group or audience engaged

- knowing how to wrap up a Q&A session in a coherent and effective manner.

And we are only getting started.

Note that we have described this skill as *managing* questions, not *answering* questions. There is a difference. We will break this down into three elements.

1. framing Q&A before questions are asked

2. diagnosing the questioner and question in real time

3. answering the question intelligently and powerfully.

DELIVERY

FRAMING

You will recall in the 12-step structure from Chapter 5, Step 6 refers to *guidelines*. Here we frame the Q&A expectations upfront.

> *In our discussions today, can you allow me 20 minutes to set the context and then we can dive into questions? This will ensure we don't get distracted along the way.*

Or

> *As we go through the agenda, please jump in with any questions or comments you may have. This is a conversation, not a presentation.*

These are frames. Your intent gives direction on when and how questions will be encouraged in the session. You can also frame types of questions:

> *The purpose of the meeting is to provide the big picture plan, and I know many of you will want to get into the detail. We will cover the detail in following meetings, so can you keep your questions at the overview level? We would like your perspectives on the big ideas. Is that clear for everyone?*

Or

> *Please feel free to challenge or attack these ideas. We must make sure we have covered everything so we are not surprised later.*

In a presentation, while the guidelines have been described, you will need to frame the Q&A session again; for example:

> *In a moment, I will take some questions.*

> *Reflect back on what you just heard ...*

What are the areas you would like more detail, or some examples or further exploration?

Can we make sure the questions are short and sharp please, so we can answer as many questions as possible?

Could you stand so we can see you, please let us know your name and where you are from.

Who would like to go first?

This provides time for people to think of questions to ask. You have also framed the nature of the questions you are looking for — clarification or going deeper — which helps participants think of their questions. The clear guidance on brevity and self-introductions benefits everyone. Finally, the 'who would like to go first?' encourages someone to ask, rather than the binary 'Are there any questions?' approach.

Framing will provide the rules and set the tone. In some situations, where there has been a lot of content, guide the group in discussion with colleagues around them; for example, 'In groups of three or four, please share your thoughts and reflections on what we have just experienced. Also come up with at least one question you would like to ask.' Then give them a few minutes to discuss. This provides time and opportunity to arrive at some thoughtful questions and contributions.

DIAGNOSING QUESTIONS

The motivations for asking questions during business meetings and presentations are multifaceted and can vary based on the individual's role, the nature of the meeting and the subject matter. Your role is to respect and track the underlying intention of questions and respond accordingly. It's a sophisticated balance between answering questions and managing questions. Whatever the reason for the question, the

DELIVERY

role of a masterful communicator is to diagnose the motives behind the question and, naturally, the question itself.

Ideally, people's questions are to better understand the material presented or the subject under discussion. Here, the person or people asking questions are simply looking for more detailed information about the topic, often wanting some examples to illustrate a point, or they may be a little confused by the logic.

It's all about clarification and understanding.

The type and quality of questions are an instant feedback tool on your delivery. If you are pitching an idea or a solution in a meeting, the questions being asked will help you gauge the effectiveness of your message. If you get lots of questions about wanting further explanation or more evidence or data, this tells you that you missed the mark.

When you are presenting or managing up, for example, a meeting with your manager's manager, expect your words to be more critically evaluated. In these situations, where the validity of your argument, reliability of data and the feasibility of proposed strategies or solutions are under intense scrutiny, the stakes are higher and more is expected of you.

If your contribution influences the decision-making process, be ready to be tested or challenged. This can be make or break. The Q&A here is *more* important than your prepared delivery.

Managing questions is all about context. We will explore the classic Q&A scenario versus a more conversation-based structure, where questions are mixed into the dialogue and conversational exchange.

What we mean by classic Q&A is that someone has spoken to an issue, updated a project or presented information, and after their input, there is a chance for questions to be asked. Generally, we find there are five reasons why people ask questions (see figure 19.1).

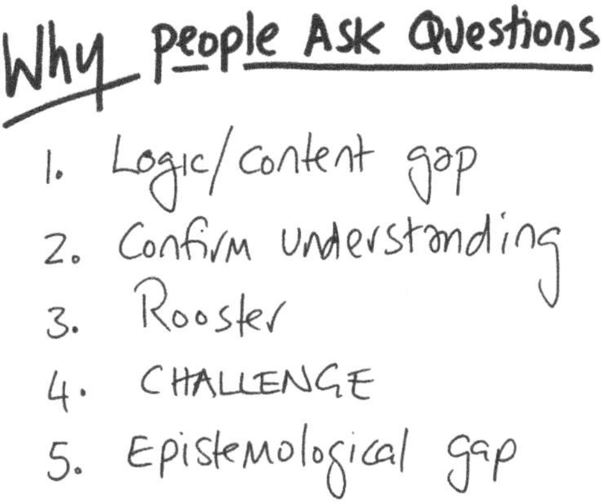

Why people Ask Questions

1. Logic/content gap
2. Confirm understanding
3. Rooster
4. CHALLENGE
5. Epistemological gap

Figure 19.1: The five reasons people ask questions

QUESTION TYPE 1: LOGIC OR CONTENT GAP

This type of question occurs frequently. Why? Because the presenter or contributor is so familiar with their topic that they make logical leaps, moving from A to D, assuming the audience already knows how B and C play out. Or they may introduce a new product to an audience and extol its virtues and benefits, but not clearly explain what it does.

Communication with assumed knowledge and logical leaps and gaps in information are all too common. Sadly, in meetings, people don't often ask for clarification because they are scared of looking foolish.

In late 2022, I was sitting in a tech conference in London, and the presenter kept mentioning NLP. In my experience, NLP stands for neuro-linguistic programming, completely unrelated to the topic on AI. I leant over to the country sales leader beside me and whispered, 'What does NLP stand for?' He paused and said, 'I'm not exactly sure.' I later discovered that it meant natural language processing, the stuff used in chatbots and virtual assistants.

This happens all the time. The sales manager who worked for the company had a content gap. Naturally, I was intrigued why he hadn't

DELIVERY

asked someone before the conference what NLP was as it was all over their website.

The way to answer this question is to close the gap, often with a quick answer. Start with a simple phrase, 'Oh, thank you, Alex, my bad, I should have been clearer ... ' before closing the gap. This encourages others to also ask questions, as you are taking responsibility for the confusion. As you should. Remember the adage: 'The meaning of your communication is the response that you get.'

I cannot count the times I've asked clients to explain an acronym, and they struggle. I am not against the use of acronyms, but I recommend always explaining what they mean in a communication situation. In the tech conference example, all the speaker had to say was, 'Let's now look at the role NLP plays in intelligent automation. As you know, NLP refers to natural language processing.'

If you find you are getting a lot of logic/content gap questions, then revisit your diagnosis and design work. You have most likely overestimated the audience's familiarity with your topic, or you have been sloppy in your logic flow. It's feedback.

Answer approach: Quick answer to ensure understanding.

QUESTION TYPE 2: CONFIRM UNDERSTANDING

'Who would like to start?' Angie asks the group, following her presentation. A hand goes up.

> *Thanks, Angie, that was insightful. Can I make sure I understand clearly what the challenge is here? Are you saying that if we use the analytics coming out of our salesforce data with more discipline and more regularly, we will have a clearer understanding of our customers and be able to plan better? Have I got that right?*

This is an example of a *confirm understanding* question. It's less of a question and more a commentary of what they've just heard or summarising the discussion they were part of.

We call this 'thinking in the mouth'. People who describe themselves as more extroverted by nature tend to talk more. They process their experience and their thinking out loud. Even at home, they will talk aloud to themselves: 'Now where did I put my keys? I came in, and I normally put them on the kitchen table. So where are they?' The thinking-aloud process helps orient and focus them.

At the risk of generalising, we find the confirm understanding type questions come from 'mouth thinkers' who are extroverts by nature. Often, they don't even finish the question, saying something like, 'It's okay, I've got it now. All good.' As they listened to themselves, the message or content fell into place.

Listen carefully to their commentary to ensure that they are on track. Most of the time, you will simply agree with their perspective, and yes, they do understand. Naturally, if they have deviated from your message or taken a detour down a track that is not useful, simply bring them back to the central theme of your communication.

Answer approach: Acknowledge and affirm if they are correct or lead them back to the content theme if they are off track.

QUESTION TYPE 3: 'ROOSTER ON THE HILL'

We use this description because it's memorable. There are some people that want to draw attention to themselves. They need it. Sometimes they crave it. Like a rooster can stand on the hill and crow loudly, some people do this display behaviour in meetings.

The risk of this label is it could be used as a pejorative. A Q&A forum creates opportunities for people to jump on their particular soapbox or to bang their favourite issue drum.

DELIVERY

On a preparation call with a client before a workshop, the client told us about one of the participants. These were her words, 'We have one of our team who loves the sound of his own voice. He always has a comment and wants to tell a story, usually about himself. Look, he is a good guy, but he can dominate.'

This is a potential 'rooster'. It's the classic 'cock a doodle do — look at me' vibe projected by some people.

The primary need a rooster has is to be acknowledged. Woven into this need is the validation attention provided by others. We all know people in our social and professional circles who sometimes desperately need to be the centre of attention.

The rooster dynamic is less about the question and more about validating the person asking the question. The rooster is more often than not motivated by good intentions. They feel comfortable and confident about speaking up and feel they are speaking on behalf of others. To reduce the rooster effect, your framing becomes important. There are two approaches:

First:

> Let's move to Q&A. Could we please focus on questions directly related to the content I've presented? We do not need commentary or reflections at this stage; we will ask for this later. So short, sharp questions please. Who would like to go first?

Second:

> The knowledge, experience and accumulated wisdom in the room is immense. Any one of you could come on the stage and we would benefit from your views and reflections on this important challenge and opportunity. We have Q&A coming up. Can we all ensure our questions are on point, and focused on the issues I've raised? Does that work for everybody? We will be looking for

deeper reflections in conversations and meetings following today's meeting. All clear? Okay, who has a question to get us started?

Even then this type of question might come into play.

Your job is *managing* questions, and managing the rooster goes with the territory. One clue that a rooster is in the room, is they often preface their question with some autobiographical information:

Thank you. Hi everyone, so happy to be here today. I think you all know me, for those who don't, my name is Felix Johnson, and I have been with the company for, oooohhh, five years now. Maybe even six! How time flies when you're having fun. Before joining this wonderful company, I had 15 years in fashion retail, including a memorable year working in Hong Kong…

None of this is relevant to the question, and a clear indication that this person needs some love.

Intervene quickly:

Thanks, Felix. Hong Kong is amazing. Can you get to the question because I can see a lot of hands in the room? Thanks, Felix.

Using their name is important. The need to be seen is often the unconscious compulsion and name acknowledgement meets this need.

It's important to ensure your energetic intention here is respect. The rooster can be an asset. They may have a story that supports your argument and outcome, so the goal here is not to stomp on the rooster, but to manage their contribution with consideration and regard.

Answer approach: Acknowledge and manage respectfully.

QUESTION TYPE 4: CHALLENGE

On a warm evening in 2000, I sat in a room with 1000+ Oracle employees, listening to the extraordinary Larry Ellison, co-founder

DELIVERY

of Oracle Corporation. The location was Auckland, on the eve of the America's Cup. He covered a range of subjects, but I will never forget one thing he said: 'If two people are in agreement, one of them is redundant.' His point was the necessity of diverse perspectives and ideas in discussions and decision-making processes. He was suggesting that if two people always agree, then they are not contributing unique viewpoints, crucial for innovation, problem-solving and avoiding groupthink in a team or organisational setting.

Challenge questions are important and necessary. Your role as an influential communicator is to encourage challenge and interrogation of the issues or topics being discussed. As we demonstrated when discussing guidelines at the beginning of the meeting, set clear ground rules for discussion. Emphasise the importance of respectful dialogue, listening and the constructive exchange of ideas, and actively invite challenges to ensure there is rigour and constructive debate around the table.

Potential tension or risk of conflict can occur when challenges are on the table or in the room. Your role is to set the energetic tone by remaining calm, regardless of how heated the discussion becomes. Keeping a level head helps in de-escalating tension and maintaining a productive atmosphere. In other words, you are managing the energetic field in the room.

You may have seen situations where a challenge question has escalated. There are no longer participants in the room, but spectators. As an influential communicator, you have a responsibility to ensure productive discourse is the name of the game. How?

In martial arts like judo or aikido, the practitioner redirects the energy of an opponent's attack instead of meeting it with equal force. Your job is to become a communication ninja, always managing the energy.

Similarly, in a meeting or a presentation, when faced with a strong, opposing viewpoint, instead of directly confronting it, you redirect this energy. Acknowledge the viewpoint, validate the emotions behind it, and then steer the conversation towards common ground or constructive outcomes.

The aikido master leverages the opponent's force rather than brute strength to gain an advantage. In a meeting, leverage comes from using persuasive facts, appealing to shared values, or highlighting mutual benefits. It's about finding that point where your argument resonates most strongly with others, with the group, not just the person asking the question.

As always, respect for all participants, even those with opposing views, fosters a more constructive and collaborative environment.

By employing these martial arts principles, you can artfully manage hostile energy in meetings. This approach not only helps in navigating conflicts but also in transforming potential discord into productive and collaborative dialogue. That's influence. On page 238, we will show you how to manage this with a step-by-step guide to managing questions.

Answer approach: Acknowledge and reframe for the whole group.

QUESTION TYPE 5: EPISTEMOLOGICAL GAP

An epistemological gap refers to a difference or a lack in understanding and knowledge between individuals or groups. Epistemology is a branch of philosophy that deals with the nature and scope of knowledge acquisition and belief. The epistemological gap is where people don't have an experience or lived memory of the topic under discussion.

Think of a city you have never been to. For the sake of an example, let's say it's Moscow. If you have been to Moscow, pick another city. Here's the question: Does Moscow exist?

DELIVERY

The answer is yes. We *know* Moscow exists because there is overwhelming evidence that it does. Photos, videos, maps, people you know who have been there, and on and on. Of course Moscow exists, however, you only really know this theoretically. You have not experienced this directly.

Would you like to learn advanced selling techniques from someone who has an incredibly successful sales career, where they make an average of $800k a year, or from a professor of sales methodology at an Ivy League school who has never sold anything in the commercial world?

One has the direct experience, or epistemology, of selling; the professor has the theoretical knowledge. The lived experience holds more credibility than someone who understands the topic intellectually.

When someone has an epistemological gap, what they need is an example or a story, not more explanation or data. They are looking for proof or evidence that your idea or suggestion is valid. In selling, the most potent tool in the sales bag are customer stories or use cases. A salesperson can make bold claims about the benefits and value of their product or solution; however, it will be the customer reference that will make it believable. Here are some examples:

Can you explain what an API is? I'm not sure how it fits into our software architecture.

How exactly does SEO impact our online marketing efforts?

I'm not familiar with the agile methodology; how does it differ from how we work now?

How do I sell to C-suite-level people?

How can I make a difference to our team culture, surely it's the manager's responsibility?

Providing examples and scenarios to these questions takes the theory and places into the real world of the questioner.

Let's use the first question on the above list as an example. Some of this structure is further explained in the next section on Q&A structure (see page 240).

Question: *Can you explain what an API is? I'm not sure how it fits into our software architecture.*

Response: *Thanks, Andy.* [**Acknowledge questioner by name.**] *This is a good opportunity to ensure we all understand this, as we use this all the time.* [**Create relevance.**] *Let me get the technical stuff out of the way first. An API, or application programming interface, is a set of rules and protocols for building and interacting with software applications. It defines how different software applications and services can communicate and share data and functionality with each other.*

Imagine you have a travel planning app on your phone. How many of you have an app like this? This app includes a feature that shows the current weather and forecast for different destinations. To provide this information, the app uses a weather reporting API.

You open the travel app and select a destination, say, Paris. What does your app now do? It sends a request to a weather service's API. This request includes the location, beautiful Paris, and the weather update. The weather service's API receives this request, processes it, fetches the relevant weather data from its database, and sends this data back to the travel app.

The travel app receives the weather data from the weather service's API and displays it to you. You can now see the current weather in Paris, along with a forecast for the next few days, right within your travel app. [**Answer using stories and examples.**] *None of*

DELIVERY

this can happen without application programming interfaces. In our business, APIs handle all the traffic between our websites, our customers, our suppliers and our employees. It manages all the traffic. Does that explain it, Andy? [**Close and check**]

Answer approach: Answer using stories and examples.

Answering questions methodology

In many situations, your answers will be quick, a simple clarification, agreement or acknowledgement to keep the process flowing. With questions with more substance, usually of the challenge and the epistemological gap variety, we recommend the following four-step structure (see figure 19.2):

1. Acknowledge the question and the questioner by name

2. Create relevance for all

3. Answer using stories and examples

4. Close, check and thank.

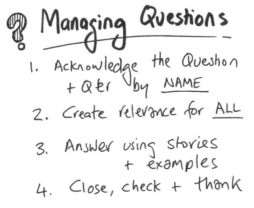

Figure 19.2: Managing questions

This structure is like a four-step dance, such as the quickstep or rumba, which is quick, slow, slow, quick in its rhythm. Two other elements included in this methodology involve *staging* and *eye contact*.

STAGING

Imagine this scenario: you are sitting in a conference room with about 50 people. A presenter has just delivered an update on a project and opens up for Q&A. Someone raises their hand ready to ask the first question.

What does the presenter typically do? They will focus on the questioner, listening. So far so good. Then this happens, the presenter invariably starts to *move towards the person asking the question*. What follows is the presenter answering the question, focusing on the questioner.

You've seen this many times. Now, what happens in the room? The energy immediately starts to decay. The dynamic has moved from a one-to-many to a one-to-one process. This reveals itself in people looking at phones, tuning out or packing up.

This also occurs in meetings. A question gets asked requiring a substantial answer, and it ends up being a conversation between two people with the rest of the meeting participants just sitting there. Q&A in both meetings and presentations needs to maintain the one-to-many dynamic to maintain attention and focus.

As we explored in anchoring, it is the counterintuitive move that will elevate your effectiveness and confidence when managing questions.

On stage, move subtly *away* from the questioner, turning your body towards the audience, as you focus and listen to the question being posed. This invites the audience to listen through you.

DELIVERY

If you are standing behind a lectern for some reason, keep your attention on the questioner and the audience, which leads us into using eye contact in the Q&A process.

EYE CONTACT

In the spirit of one-to-many communication, where you focus your attention matters. The audience or participants cue off you. Where your attention flows, the audience goes.

Once the question is asked, your attention and focus shifts onto the room or those around the table to ensure you maintain the energy needed to keep engagement high. Your response is always to the many, only in the close do you return to the questioner to check and thank.

Q&A structure

Step 1: Acknowledge the question and the questioner by name

This sounds straightforward, yet there is one important distinction to add to your acknowledging of the questioner.

Listen to interviews on the radio or podcasts, where the rules are an interviewer poses a question, giving the person the opportunity to respond. How often do you hear, 'That's a good question'? There are variations of this, such as:

That's a great question.

I'm glad you asked that question.

That's a very good question.

That's an excellent question.

I was listening to NewsRadio, and a journalist was interviewing the mayor of a town in Queensland about a fire threatening the town. The journalist asked, 'Are the citizens of the town worried about the fires?' The mayor responded with, 'That's an excellent question...' No, it isn't. It's the question anyone would expect a journalist to ask.

The reflex response of 'that's a good question', or similar, comes across as formulaic or, worse, insincere. At best, it provides some thinking time, but there are more elegant and effective ways to implement this step.

Using the person's name is respectful and builds immediate connection. In meetings and with groups you work with regularly, you will likely know their names. In presentation contexts, with bigger groups, invite people to share their name before asking the question. If they don't, ask them their name before moving to acknowledgement.

Here are some examples:

Thank you, Lin. Lin has raised an important question for all of us to consider...

Ahhh, Chris has hit the nail on the head with this question...

Ahmed, thank you, I was hoping this question would be asked...

Okay, Kristina, your question leads us into some very interesting territory...

Your acknowledgement of the question goes way beyond the reflexive 'good question' response, and demonstrates a thoughtful and considered reflection. The person answering the question feels respected and linking the question to relevance is cleaner. The purpose of acknowledgement is to bridge into Step 2.

Step 2: Create relevance for all

The person asking the question has a reason why they asked the question. Your job is to now connect their question to the topic or issue at hand, and to frame the question so everyone in the room can buy into the answer.

Without relevance there is no motive for anyone to listen to the answer, except out of politeness. Remember, your attention remains with the group, not just the individual who asked the question. There are a number of ways we can create relevance.

OBVIOUS RELEVANCE

Often, the relevance is as simple as saying, 'Jason's question is something we all need to consider, because it affects everyone around this table.' Here, you are simply telling participants to 'listen up'.

If you notice that the question itself is sparking interest and attention, then the relevance step is very straightforward. Simply asking, 'Am I right in thinking Jason's question is something we all want the answer to?' serves the purpose.

CREATE RELEVANCE

Many times the question is only relevant to a few people, maybe only the person asking the question. It could be something like, 'Our team provided support and we respond to requests, so what you have shared doesn't really impact us at all. Does that mean we should just wait and see what happens?' At one logical level the answer to this question could be 'yes'.

However, the question affords the opportunity to encourage people not to be passive, but to get involved. Your job is to create relevance. In this case you could respond with:

Amy does remind everyone here that we all play different, but critical roles in this project. Thank you, Amy. And for some teams we will be called on at different times. Amy, your team is a case in point, and can we all recognise that we need to keep our eyes on progress and keep our teams involved? Even if their contribution could be months down the track? We don't want any surprises. Or being under prepared when the time comes, do we? So, how will we stay informed every step of the way?

In this case, Amy was suggesting she and her team can exempt themselves from the process, and your creation of relevance re-engages her, and everyone else, into the importance of staying informed.

REFRAME RELEVANCE

Questions of a challenging nature have the potential to shift the energy in the meeting or room, to turn up the heat. People can smell the potential conflict or tension in the air. Absorbing the challenge becomes the goal.

'This project is significantly behind schedule and over budget. How can you justify these delays and additional costs?' asks Clyde at the conclusion of the project status update.

This is a challenge question, which, at face value, is attacking the credibility of the presenter or speaker at the meeting. It's provocative, and the instinct to get defensive is understandable. Defensiveness will only lay the foundations for further attack.

- ◆ Step 1: Acknowledge: 'Thank you Clyde, for addressing the progress of our project. This is important for all of us to understand.'

DELIVERY

◆ Step 2: Reframe relevance: 'Clyde's question rightly asks how we can justify the current state. It's important to recognise that this project is not just a routine task — it's a ground-breaking initiative that sets new standards in our industry. Can any of you recall a time when a project did not go exactly to plan? How do we make sense of this? Let's explore what we know so we can align on how to move forward productively.'

The key is the last line. Moving from justification to progressing forward. This is more useful. It reframes the relevance for the room and moves attention away from having to explain.

This might be considered a spin doctor move, and it is certainly what politicians do when getting tough questions — always spinning to the positive or the narrative they are pushing.

In this case, the objective is to take the question and let it be used to inform a productive discussion. The question 'how do you justify?' is a credibility challenge, suggesting that the person should step down or get out of the building. It's not a productive question. The intent is hostile. The reframe turns down the heat and allows space for a more considered and intelligent reflection on what to do next.

Having acknowledged and ensured the question is valuable for everyone involved, it's time to move to the answer.

Step 3: Answer using stories and examples

As we have discovered earlier, the experiential gap, the epistemological gap, suggests that the person asking the question has no reference, or lived experience, that allows them to make sense of the subject under discussion.

For example, the advent of AI has a vast array of unknowns. When talking about the rise of intelligent augmented reality and robotic automations, everyone is looking for ways of understanding this. Theory is one thing, but 'please connect this to my real world' is the question they are asking. How? Use stories, examples or scenarios.

Same thing with challenge questions. The challenge is made, and stories, examples and scenarios can move attention into a productive space rather than sparring with words.

We will plunge into the magical world of storytelling in the next chapter; however, it becomes imperative to keep your story library well stocked when going into Q&A sessions.

Epistemological gap and challenge questions emerge from the inability to connect the theoretical dots. Data explain and logically argue a case, but are not an experience. It can make rational sense; however, most people are looking for meaning and connection to their 'real world'. We go back to Bernice McCarthy and the 4-Mat model on page xix. Ideas lock into consciousness if they relate to the lived reality of the people in the room. Full stop. Your answers must meet this need.

Using the example of Clyde's challenging question above, the answer could be:

> *It's important to recognise that this project is not just a routine task; it's a ground-breaking initiative that sets new standards in our industry. We've encountered some unforeseen challenges, which are typical in pioneering ventures.*

This is the place for a story. Drawing from the company's history is the best bet. Every organisation will have a story of a project that started badly, missed targets, but emerged as a success. Importantly, lessons were learnt, experience was gained.

Generic examples can also be found; for example, the construction cost of the Sydney Opera House was originally estimated at

AU$7 million, but the final cost soared to AU$102 million, and the project was completed ten years late. Despite these challenges, the Opera House is now an iconic landmark and a major tourist attraction, and has brought billions of tourist dollars to the Australian economy.

The story leads to closing your answer, linking the story to the outcome; for example:

> *These challenges have given all of us invaluable learning experiences that are enhancing our team's capabilities. We're not just building a project; we're developing a new benchmark for quality and performance in our field. The insights and improvements we're gaining already are improving this project, but will also streamline our future projects, saving time, saving money. It's been painful, of course, and we are adjusting as we go.*

The story provides the social proof of history, the potential for a positive outcome, and a reference to highlight that many, if not most, innovation projects struggle to stay on plan and budget.

Plan for challenge questions. Imagine worst possible scenarios and be armed and ready with powerful examples and proof through use cases, customer stories and the like.

In 2012, we were facilitating a leadership offsite with partners of a major consulting firm. A question similar to the challenge question was raised. The response from the senior partner presenting the project update was something like:

> *You are right, John. The project has blown out beyond what we hoped. We've all been there. Plans do not always play out perfectly. How many of us have done renovations to our homes? Some of you have built your own houses. Did they go to plan? How many months over did it go? And over budget by how much? John, I know you have recent history with this.*

Challenge beautifully met.

DEFER AND DEFLECT

Not every question requires an answer. Some questions are so weird, irrelevant or specific, that a group forum is not the place to provide an answer. As always, you need to assess the benefit to the audience.

Examples of questions to defer or deflect:

♦ personal issues

♦ HR problems or scenario

♦ it's outside your expertise

♦ specific customer or privacy situations

♦ simply don't understand the question and don't have time to unpack the meaning.

The response is straightforward. 'Amy, can we discuss this immediately after the meeting. We will need more time. Is that okay? Thanks.'

Occasionally people blurt a question and immediately regret it. Save them. They know that their question is either irrelevant, inappropriate or both. Move on quickly and leave it behind, reducing any time or focus on the person who asked the question.

DON'T PRETEND TO KNOW

Never pretend or waffle an answer. Everyone will notice this and your credibility will be tarnished, compromising everything you have shared with them. Provide a safety net in setting up the Q&A by framing what you can and cannot answer.

In a moment, we will have time for Q&A. I need to let you know I may not be able to answer all your questions. There is detail and specifics that are not in my area, so if questions do arise like this, I will point you to the right person to ask. Also, if some questions are dealing with issues that are confidential, you will understand that I cannot discuss them in the meeting. I'll endeavour to do my best though. Who would like to start?

If a question is asked that you cannot answer, simply acknowledge that you don't know.

The objective here is to hold your ground. The moment you diminish your authority by being overly apologetic, or embarrassed, it will immediately reduce your credibility and impact.

If you have framed your content well, established guidelines regarding types of questions, and acknowledged you may not be across all the detail, it is unlikely you will be hit with questions that could take you down roads you don't want to go.

Step 4: Close, check and thank

Having answered the question, no matter how brief or long the answer is, always respectfully check back with the person who asked the question.

The key step here is 'check'. How often have you experienced a Q&A when the question wasn't answered? You might have experienced a situation where your question was poorly managed or simply not answered at all. This becomes your abiding memory of the event. 'She didn't answer my question, did you notice?' is what you mutter to your colleagues after the meeting.

It's as simple as saying things like ...

Does that answer your question, Clyde? Thank you.

Is that clearer, Jane? Thanks.

I trust that gives you something to work with Chloé? I'm glad. Thanks.

Can you work with that Peter?

If you see confusion on their faces, or receive a shrugged nod, you might want to go back to clarify. Time and context are factors here. It is okay to say, 'There is more we need to go into here. Marianne, can we catch up afterwards?' to ensure you don't get deep into the quicksand of specifics that will not be relevant to everyone in attendance.

In workshop situations, you will have time to go deeper with answers. The Socratic Method, named after the Greek philosopher Socrates, is a form of teaching and discussion based on asking and answering questions to stimulate critical thinking and illuminate ideas. This method is an excellent way of using questions to go deeper into ideas and insights.

Tim Chilvers, one of our master facilitators, demonstrated this superbly, in Brisbane in 2017. We were working with a credit union, and one of the participants, Julie, asked a question related to leading people through difficult changes. Tim's answer was a deep dive into a very useful framework we use called 'managing the pit'.

Tim used the first steps of acknowledging Julie and creating relevance, before exploring the model. Everyone was enthralled. Notes were being taken. There was a breakout group activity thrown in. Fifty minutes later, Tim summarised the benefits of the framework and the skills linked to implementing it, and said, 'So, does that answer your question, Julie?' Julie was staggered. 'Um, yes, more than I could have ever hoped.'

In most cases the managing questions framework will be used in a standard Q&A session, but, if time allows, it can allow for deep work in step 3.

DELIVERY

This four-step structure, supported by keeping your attention on everyone in attendance with eye contact, is a superb management tool for Q&A, and particularly where there are differing points of view.

No surprise — it takes practice.

Wrapping up Q&A

Q&A is typically the final phase of a presentation or meeting. It's the chance to tie up loose ends, mollify concerns and bring more clarity to issues being discussed or explored.

This affords an opportunity to remind the group of your call to action and close. Ideally, you can also include a summary of the questions you just managed.

> *In closing, I want to thank Clyde, Julie, Jane, Chloé, Kristina, Chris and, of course, Lin for getting us started. Please feel free to catch up with me later, or drop me an email if you have any questions or ideas you would like to share.*

Demonstrating that you remembered everyone's names, and acknowledging everyone again, is a powerful demonstration of your care and focus.

Relationship wrap-up

Building, maintaining and developing the relationship dynamics around the table or in the room is key to creating the conditions for effective communication to take place, and influence to occur.

We come back to the power of respect. When this is authentic, it is felt and appreciated. When people feel respected, they lift. Performance improves, anxiety is reduced and the spirit is encouraged.

Simple things like using names, making eye contact, paying attention, using questions, and managing questions effectively is all wrapped up in healthy relationships in the workplace. Lead by example.

DELIVERY

CHAPTER 20
STORY

At this stage of our journey, we would all agree that effective communication stands as a cornerstone of a successful career.

Where does story and storytelling fit into the scheme of things? Evidently, it fits in everywhere! 'Story' and 'narrative' are almost compulsory words in the workplace these days.

We need to take ownership of the narrative. [**Who owns it now?**]

Our 2030 vision tells the story of our organisation, our people and our customers. [**Does it?**]

Our narrative takes our customers on an authentic experiential journey. [**You mean buying stuff?**]

We need to tell our story better. [**You mean effective marketing?**]

Tell me your story. [**Job interview?**]

While the word 'story' is thrown around quite loosely, the reality is stories are powerful when used with precision and purpose.

Poor use of stories will confuse or bore people. Think about stories as your argument or business case. Stories are real-world evidence to validate and support your content. If you show a graph indicating a drop in sales, a story from a customer as to why they are reluctant to buy is more convincing and insightful than the descending steps on a graph.

To enhance your leadership abilities and connect more profoundly with your colleagues and your teams, storytelling emerges as a powerful tool. The significance of storytelling in the workplace, and exploring its utility is our final piece of the PAVERS® elements.

The power of storytelling

We are all products of stories.

Your family history, the culture you were born into, the ethnic group, the socioeconomic circumstances you grew up in, not to mention religion, gender, health circumstances, along with many other factors become the stories you were raised in.

Values, beliefs, world views, sense of identity were all evident in the stories you heard as you shared meals and played with siblings or friends. Different stories were read to you before sleep, were projected on TV and other screens, and were introduced into your education experience. At its core, storytelling transcends mere information exchange. When you first entered the workforce, you learnt from stories.

What's the boss like?

How do things happen around here?

Who are the people I can trust? Who do I need to be wary of?

Do people like working here?

What's Jenny like? She seems super competitive?

These questions will lead to stories, anecdotes, examples.

Stories weave facts with emotions, making messages more relatable and memorable. Stories are human. Work is full of situations where data and directives are omnipresent, and stories will humanise interactions, ensuring you bring engaging and persuasive contributions to meetings and presentations.

Let's jump into *why* stories are so important and critical in how you communicate. Stories convince, illuminate, illustrate, engage and validate.

Stories for vision, mission and values

When we first engage with potential clients, we ask what vision, mission and values are defining their business and organisation. It will be no surprise that, more often than not, they struggle to articulate the words.

The vision is invariably a quest for value, contribution, achievement and the like. Values tend to be things like respect, integrity, teamwork, customer obsession, unity and so on. It's easy to get a little jaded by these, as we see them splashed across every customer website. A Google search will show you that the most common values, across all industries, are teamwork, customer-focused, respect, integrity, passion, and innovation. Are these similar to your workplace?

These are important things to value. The risk is they are not connected to meaning, and, if that is the case, can breed cynicism. 'Respect? That's bullshit for a start. The managers here show zero respect for their teams.'

The role of a leader, or a person of influence, is to turn these words into meaning. It's almost a cliché to refer to people like Steve Jobs of Apple, who was a master storyteller. Excuse the pun, but Jobs drove

Apple's core values with fierceness and relentless consistency. Have you ever opened an Apple product? The unboxing experience is a joy. That is a result of the values of elegance, simplicity and innovation that drove Apple in the early days, and still do.

Jobs' product launches were legendary, and he often wove stories about how a new device wasn't just a piece of technology but a key to unlocking personal potential.

I recall the leader of the Commonwealth Bank retail division, Ross McEwan, talking about individual employee's roles, and tying them to the company's commitment to employee welfare and customer satisfaction. The employees loved these stories. They were relatable and showed how values link to everyday behaviour

In your workplace, what are the values promoted by the leaders? Do they reside in your head and heart? If not, why not? As a masterful communicator, find stories in your own life, and in the experiences of your colleagues, to identify the stories that exemplify the values.

Anyone can say courage is one of our values. What does that mean? Give me an example. Tell me a story.

Stories about change and overcoming resistance

Change management is a place where storytelling proves invaluable. Most of us are resistant to change. Even trying to give up a bad habit is difficult, let alone dealing with the change all around us. Well-crafted stories can ease this resistance, providing examples that help people understand and embrace change. Here's an example:

Alison, at 46, decided it was time to make a change in her life. She had been happily divorced for three years and her son had moved into a share house. Alison thought, 'time for a new adventure.'

She applied for and was offered a role in the Office of Sport, NSW, meaning a move to Sydney from Melbourne, where she had been living for 20 years. She could not remember the last time she felt so excited about a challenge.

After a big party with family and friends to farewell her, she got into her car, packed to the gills, for the nine-hour drive to a new job, a new city and a new life.

It was three weeks later, sitting alone in her apartment in Cremorne, with glimpses of the harbour, that she felt she had made the biggest mistake of her life.

She did not know anyone. Sydney seemed harsh and aggressive compared to Melbourne. The job was challenging, as expected, but people treated her with cool regard, like the stranger she was.

She wondered if it would be ridiculous to give up and make the nine-hour trip back home.

What Alison was experiencing was 100 per cent predictable. Every major change we make in our lives starts with high energy before sliding into 'the pit'. Alison is not alone.

Embedded in the story is the relatable experience of making a dramatic change. The point of the story is to acknowledge that change is initially exciting, however, there is the difficult transition awaiting. The story serves as link or bridge into the topic exploring the psychology of change.

Find stories of 'change journeys' that can help people understand their experience, or to prepare them for challenges ahead. Draw from your own experiences. We have all experienced our own pit moments in our personal and professional lives. This is the power of the human story.

DELIVERY

Stories for learning

As you might guess, we use stories in training and development to connect theory with the real world.

Storytelling is an essential part of our early development. It is through stories that we learn about language, emotions and the world around us. From nursery rhymes to bedtime tales, storytelling played a crucial role in fostering our imagination, cognitive skills, and emotional intelligence. We learnt about good and bad, threat and safety, courage and carefulness. Big bad wolf, anyone?

Hopefully, as a child, you were transported to magical worlds, mythical creatures, and fantastical adventures. Stories ignite our imaginations and encourage creative thinking. As we listen or engage in storytelling, we envision vivid pictures in our minds, creating our own unique interpretations, linking to our own real-world experience.

If you are mentoring someone or providing constructive feedback, using stories becomes an excellent device for showing the way, providing living examples, and allowing the person to make their own connections and meaning.

At time of writing this, I'm mentoring a senior leader based in Dubai. She is a formidable presence and has built an extraordinary career. She is experiencing the glass ceiling phenomenon so many women leaders still experience. Her 'force of nature' style tends to intimidate some of the men she reports to, despite the incredible success she and her team deliver to the company. Instead of giving advice, I have been using stories of accomplished women, who faced more difficult situations and succeeded. She then references the stories in how she will alter and refine her approach.

Stories for building teams

Google, a client of ours, is known for its innovative management practices, and encourages work teams to share stories during meetings, fostering a culture of openness and trust. These are a mix of personal and business stories, creating a conversational experience rather than a formal meeting.

During these meetings, updates about the company's projects and future plans are shared in a story format. People are asked to share personal stories about the work they are doing, particularly where they may be struggling and needing support. Googlers, as they call themselves, love these meetings, finding them engaging and relatable. Everyone is given the opportunity to share their stories, which leads to the culture of openness and transparency everyone hopes for in the workplace.

What is the story of the team you work with? When are stories shared? How can you use stories to bring life to the work your team is doing at least once a week?

Storytelling in crisis management

Back in 2010, Qantas faced a major crisis when one of their A380 planes had an engine explosion shortly after take-off. It was hugely scary for everyone on board. Qantas is famous for being the safest airline on the planet. This was a serious incident that could severely damage the airline's reputation.

The CEO at the time, Alan Joyce, immediately grounded the entire A380 fleet until they could ensure the safety of these planes. No hesitation. No explanation. The entire fleet was grounded.

What stood out was how Qantas used storytelling to manage this crisis. Passengers who were on the flight expressed their feelings and experiences to cameras and journalists with the *encouragement* of Qantas. The crew members who handled the emergency landing professionally and ensured everyone's safety were applauded and their stories were told.

Qantas immediately created a series of videos and blog posts providing updates on the investigation and the steps they were taking to prevent such incidents in the future. These stories helped humanise the company and showed their commitment to passenger safety.

As a result? Qantas managed to maintain their customers' trust. This transparent communication and effective use of storytelling played a crucial role in this.

The sad reality is that this Qantas story is an exception. In recent times, a major telecommunications company in Australia lost trust across their entire customer base. The press smashed them for security breaches and outages. They lost control of the story. Their CEO is gone, the scapegoat in the crises. All because they did not manage the narrative, and were not open and transparent in their storytelling.

When things go wrong, as they always do, find the story that acknowledges what happened, be honest about the effects, and assure stakeholders that lessons are being learnt as the situation is being handled. In crisis situations, *over* communicate.

Have you been stuck on a plane or train when there is no communication? All you want is to know what is going on. Keep us informed. What is the story? The stress and anxiety of *not* knowing something is *greater* than knowing.

Customer stories

Stories are a powerful tool for influencing and, even more powerfully, selling. Every organisation will have hundreds of customer and client stories, both good and bad.

Across the world are tabloid TV programs that share horror stories of how people got ripped off or were treated badly by businesses. These stories can damage brands and businesses profoundly. Just one bad customer story can destroy a small business. Stories matter. These stories invariably end with a grovelling apology and a promise to compensate the angry customer who had to resort to going to the media to solve their problem.

Every time you rate a service on Tripadvisor, Airbnb or anywhere you can leave a review, the score and story you tell will influence potential customers. It's your micro-story. I will often ignore the five-star ratings and look for the one-star reviews to see what their story was. One bad review can cancel a bunch of positive ones.

These stories reflect the experiences and perspectives of real customers. At the heart of every customer story is an authentic, relatable human experience. When potential customers hear or read about others who have benefited from a product or service, they are likely to see themselves in similar scenarios. This helps them understand the value proposition on a deeper level and also creates an emotional connection with the brand.

The US marketing expert Seth Godin says, 'Marketing is no longer about the stuff that you make, but about the stories you tell.'

Customer stories are the ultimate social proof. Robert Cialdini identified this psychological phenomenon where people conform to the behaviour of the many. If you walk down a street full of different restaurants, and you notice that business is booming and the restaurants appeared packed with patrons, then you come across a restaurant that is empty. Do you go in? Of course not. Social proof tells you that this restaurant is a dud. People vote with their feet.

Your customer stories must be genuine, compelling and well-crafted. Highlight the challenges that customers faced, how the product or service helped overcome those challenges, and the resulting benefits. The narrative needs to be engaging, easy to understand and resonate with the participants in the meeting or presentation.

Customer stories hold immense power in selling and influencing. They humanise the brand, build trust, provide social proof and offer valuable insights.

Powerful stories always have five elements. They:

1. are real

2. are relevant to the audience

3. are simple and easy to follow

4. make you feel something

5. have an explicit point and link.

Real stories

Authenticity is the foundation of trust and connection. The most effective stories are real. There are thousands of stories you can draw from your life alone. Organisations and businesses are creating and experiencing stories every day. Sharing real experiences, even vulnerabilities, is powerful.

If you have ever read the travel experiences of the master storyteller Bill Bryson, you will laugh at his simple observations of everyday life as he walks through various cities or countryside. At a literary lunch in Sydney in 2014, he spoke to the 400 people, keeping us all engrossed and laughing, when he held up a notebook and said, 'This has allowed me to put all my kids through college and to buy a few houses here and there, and to have an almost embarrassingly comfortable life.' He explained that he carries a notebook wherever he goes, and simply records what he sees, what he experiences and his quirky observations. Opening the notebook, he said:

> *For example, this morning at breakfast in my hotel, the young waiter, an eyebrow ring of awkward size dominating his pimpled face, asked if I wanted a coffee. I said 'No, but I would like a pot of tea.' He walked away but my tea never arrived. Five minutes later the bejewelled youth passed my table, and I caught his attention and asked him if my pot of tea was arriving soon. He looked blankly at me and said, 'I don't know, I only deal with coffee.'*

Bill showed us the pages of his notebook covered in his scrawl, 'Will I use this story? I don't know, but I loved the fact that this guy stuck so enthusiastically to his job description.'

Bill Bryson demonstrates that stories surround us all the time. To build a 'story library', become aware of what happens around you, no matter how mundane or ordinary, because there could be a lesson or story to carry your message and support your communication outcome.

As I write this in November 2023, I reflect on a Zoom program I delivered with 30 people from across Europe. Our workshops are interactive, and we encourage contributions and questions, when I heard a voice, 'Colin, can I make a comment?' As I scanned the boxes on my computer screen, I found the person speaking. His camera was on, but all we could see was his forehead. His screen was tilted at an angle that meant we were all enjoying the wall and ceiling of his lounge room but could only see his well combed hair bobbing as he spoke. I had stopped listening because, like everyone on the workshop, I was so distracted by the sight of this animated head without a face.

That is a story. What does it mean? How could I use this story? Where would this story be used? It could illustrate the principle 'it's not what you say, it's how you say it', or it could be linked to the idea of self-awareness, knowing the impression you are making, either live or virtual.

Will I use this story? Maybe. But it's now in the library, waiting for the perfect moment where I can take it out and use it in a conversation, at a meeting or during a presentation.

Relevance

Relevance is everything. Tailor the story to your audience and context. The more relatable your story, the more effective it will be.

One June evening in 2023, I was on a Zoom coaching call with a finance manager based in a Scandinavian software company. A quiet, studious, undemonstrative guy, he epitomised the contained energy of people from that part of the world. He was preparing for a major board meeting, where his recommendation of whether they should sell the company would be an influential factor in how the board was going to proceed. He needed to be bold, confident and convincing. By nature, he is introverted, undemonstrative and, yes, quiet.

He realised what he had to do. He could not hide behind his introverted persona. We rehearsed his 'extrovert' to demonstrate conviction and confidence in why he was recommending not selling. His logic and business case were convincing, and his passionate, expressive way of stating his case would reinforce this. He also needed a story. We shaped a story about two employees who had been with the company for over ten years, and how they believed in the purpose and value of the company.

After the board meeting, he reflected on the experience.

> *It felt unnatural at first, then I realised it wasn't unnatural at all, it was that I was simply unfamiliar with expressing myself this way. And it was necessary. The board went with my recommendation and acknowledged my passionate defence. In fact, it felt kind of liberating. What convinced them was the story. It beautifully supported the business case.*

Stories are very persuasive in supporting any relevance argument or case you make.

Keep it simple

We probably all have a relative who, at family events, particularly if there is some chardonnay inspiration, will launch into some story, loaded with detail, side roads, excursions into irrelevance and looming sense that there will be no end, let alone a point. They go on and on and on and on. And on.

Short, punchy, powerful stories have a simple narrative. They are easy to understand and create space for the listeners' imagination to fill in the gaps.

The principle at play is juuuuuust enough detail. You need to say the last sentence out loud to appreciate its meaning. Storytelling in a work context serves a purpose; it is not used solely to entertain.

Feel something

Because stories invariably include humans, they are, by definition, emotive. This will ensure *emotional connection*. Connecting the head to the heart and gut builds a full body experience. Taking dry content, data and information and connecting it to the human experience leads

DELIVERY

to this most critical element in influence: meaning. When something is meaningful, it is felt. Emotions drive our behaviour. Data give us a rational reason to do something; emotions turn the rational into experience and energy.

Point and link

An effective story always has a *point*, and always needs to *link* to the subject under discussion. Think of this as a 'call to action', where the story inspires or encourages. Stories need to inspire people to feel, think and act differently. We'll dissect the point and link approach more thoroughly on page 275.

Storytelling is not just an ancillary skill, or something to include in your communication occasionally. Stories need to be tactically and intelligently integrated into your communication approach in every work context.

Stories are a fundamental tool in effective communication. Stories bridge the gap between dry data and meaningful interaction, foster a culture of openness and learning, and effectively drive change and innovation.

In an age where information overload is the norm, the ability to tell a compelling story makes the difference between being heard and being overlooked. To elevate your communication skills, mastering the art of storytelling is not just valuable — it's essential.

Story structure

Building your storytelling muscle requires an understanding of where stories come from, how they are used, and the depth of design needed to make your stories powerful and persuasive.

We will look at two typical story structures before introducing you to something we call 'magic formula stories'.

The hero's story

Every hero journey starts with a challenge and this is why, in a work context, the hero story is often seen in sales.

The hero's story is found in every culture and has been central to oral traditions across the world. Joseph Campbell's wonderful book, *Hero with a thousand faces*, explored the patterns found in narratives around the world.[25] The formula found in myths and legends follows stages, including the call to the action, facing trials and danger, feeling lost and desperate, finding support and wisdom before returning to the ordinary world.

Anyone who has gone on a gap year, backpacking with a few measly dollars in their pocket, will experience their own version of the hero's journey.

The hero story in a work context is often seen in sales. For example, here is a story where I have changed the company names for confidentiality reasons.

The hero is Alex, an account executive for ABCTech, a software company headquartered in The Netherlands, who takes on the challenge of saving an account, an insurance company called EuroInsurance. (We spent many minutes coming up with these company names.)

Here is the story, see if you can track the hero journey pathway.

- The ordinary world

- Call to adventure

- Doubt

◆ Guidance from a mentor

◆ Accepting the challenge

◆ Facing the dragons and demons

◆ Tipping point: seizing the opportunity

◆ Success

◆ Lessons learnt

Alex, an account executive at ABCTech, is known for her expertise in handling complex clients. She is respected by her colleagues for her work ethic, her optimism and her ability to build great customer relationships. When people think of Alex, the first word most use is 'respect'. At 28 years old, and new to the sales game, she is good at what she does. [**ordinary world**]

Alex's manager, Maria, calls Alex and says 'We have a problem. We could lose one of major accounts. Can you step in?' Alex is assigned a high-stakes client in the insurance industry. This client, crucial for ABCTech's portfolio, is on the brink of shifting to Microsoft due to perceived shortcomings in ABCTech's solutions. [**call to adventure**]

Alex is reluctant to take on this challenge, feeling it might be a lost cause. 'It's too late', she tells one of her colleagues, 'I'm not superwoman! I don't know the client. Why the hell would they listen to me?' [**doubt**]

Maria calls Alex again. Maria spends an hour briefing Alex on the client, the history, the personalities, as well as industry insights and suggestions on strategic client management. [**guidance from a mentor**]

Alex accepts. Everest awaits. **[accepting the challenge]**

Her first meeting with three executives from EuroInsurance is less than successful. The chief technology officer is borderline rude. 'Are you the last hope to rescue this account, Alex? We are going with Microsoft; we will not renew. Case closed.' [**facing the dragons and demons**]

This pale, stale male did not know Alex. It was exactly this sort of attitude that lit her fire. She threw herself into deep analysis, discovering systemic problems; a history of wasted investment in technology; and how Microsoft was a cheaper option, but nowhere near what EuroInsurance needed. Microsoft was offering a bicycle, ABCTech was offering a high-powered racing machine.

Alex asked for one more meeting. The three smug executives attended again. Forty-five minutes later, the chief technology officer said this, 'Alex, let me apologise for what I said in our last meeting. What you have just shown us has forced me to rethink our approach. This was illuminating and brilliantly delivered. Thank you.' [**tipping point**]

This was the turning point. There was still work to be done. The CEO nearly upset things at the last minute, but Alex was on fire and fully focused.

The deal was closed on the last day of the quarter, and is the biggest deal in Alex's career to date. [**success**]

Maria, at the close of the quarter, told the entire sales team, 'Alex has given us a template on how to keep customers. Her example is something we can all benefit from. Thank you, Alex. Job well done!' [**lessons learnt**]

This story follows the hero's journey structure step-by-step.

These hero stories are not only inspirational, but they also serve as models of possibility, encouraging others to take up the challenge and become a hero themselves. They are best used in presentations, workshops and offsite meetings.

Three-act framework

In the workplace, the three acts guide how you put the story together. This is a simple and effective way of structuring short, punchy stories. No surprises — this divides your story into three parts:

1. set-up (introducing characters and the situation)

2. confrontation/situation (what happens: drama, challenge, conflict?)

3. resolution (where things are resolved).

You will see the three-act framework being used many times throughout a movie or TV show.

A young woman walks down the street, late at night, and it's raining. [**act one**]

A stranger appears in the distance, looking threatening. He has a scarf wrapped around his face.

The woman is nervous, scared. The stranger gets closer. What does she do? Run? Attack? Scream? [**act two**]

The stranger is just two strides from her, 'Oh my god, there you are, I was so worried', says the man. It's her partner, out looking for her. They embrace. [**act three**]

We have seen variations of this thousands of times. But how does this apply to work-based communication?

Set-up: We had a very difficult conversation with the risk team. John was looking very annoyed, and the vibe in the meeting was pretty tense.

Confrontation/situation: He accused Melanie and me of overstepping our authority. He almost shouted, 'You have no right to make these decisions without talking to us first!' I know John can be quite vocal across the group, and I was not going to let him accuse us of professional negligence.

Resolution: I showed him the copies of the three emails we had sent, along with the attachments, asking for a response. I explained that, despite our three requests, we had heard nothing, and we had to make a decision because of the deadline. I said, 'John, we are all fighting for our lives on this, and stuff can get lost along the way. Apologies for not making further efforts to bring this to your attention.' That did it. He was fine after that.

But the story alone does not make it 'magical'. The magic lies in your ability to *link* the story to meaning, making the story relevant to your audience or participants, where the story does the heavy lifting in achieving the outcome.

DELIVERY

Magic formula stories

As we have seen, there are various ways of putting a story together. The power of an effective story is building the connection of the story to the issue and outcome at hand. We call this linking.

The magic refers to the moment when people get it! The 'A-ha!' moment when they understand, recognise implications and are already thinking about applications (see figure 20.1, overleaf).

Figure 20.1: Magic formula stories

There are three phases to using magic formula stories:

1. Event

2. Point

3. Link to outcome or message.

The event

The three-act structure could apply here. In the work context, incorporate the following details:

- When did this occur or take place (time, location)?

- Where was the location (city, building, place space)?

- Who was involved (characters, names, appearances)?

- What happened? (Describe the scenario)

When a story is being told, the listener is always checking for veracity. Is this true? You will hear comedians preface their stories with 'I swear this is true ... ' because stories based on reality and lived experience carry power.

Small but significant details ensure your story is believable. Consider the difference:

I was talking to a client once, and they told me that there is a lot of anxiety about AI replacing jobs.

Versus

Two months ago, the chief people officer of an insurance company in Melbourne told me, 'I have had so many people raise the AI issue, including our accountants and legal people. 'Will I lose my job?' is the question I hear all the time now.' She is not alone.

Which story feels true? The first version lacks the small details needed to convey authenticity. The second version has when, where, who and what outlined in one sentence.

When? Two months ago

Where? Melbourne

Who? Female insurance company CPO

What? Staff talking to her about AI threats

This 15-second story introduces the broad concerns about technology replacing a swathe of jobs, particularly traditional white-collar roles, and gives credence and authority through the words of a chief people officer.

A lack of specificity raises the question of veracity.

DELIVERY

Last Friday, I met the headmaster of a renowned Melbourne private school in a school building that was over 100 years old. He arrived in the meeting room, dressed impeccably in a grey suit, and his six-foot-plus frame filled the room with quiet authority. His firm handshake, and deep voice indicted that when he spoke, people listened.

The little details paint the picture without *all* the brushstrokes. The extraordinary ability of the human imagination to fill in the spaces is why stories work so well.

Once we have determined when and where stories will be employed in your design, the 'magic' use of the story lies in your ability to make a salient point, and then link seamlessly to the outcome. That outcome could be establishing relevance, overcoming FODs, validating your idea, supporting your data, considering the future.

The point

A story can have many points. Children's fairy tales, such as *Little Red Riding Hood*, is loaded with points. Stranger danger; be alert; things are not what they seem; if you see a predator eating your grandmother in front of your eyes, that might be a reason to feel some anxiety about your own safety.

In July 2015, we were running a training workshop in Sydney, and we asked participants to leave the building and find a story. Olivia returned 40 minutes later. Here's her story:

I left the building and stepped onto a crowded George Street. It's hot today and everyone was looking a little worn down by the heat. I decided to cross the road, and at the traffic lights I pressed that silver button thing, it supposedly changes the lights. Waiting for the little green man icon. The person just behind me also pressed the button. As did three or four other people. They saw me press the thing, so why did they feel like they had to? Did they have the mystical power? Did their finger possess the secret to controlling the lights?

From this one story, the group came up with several workable points.

◆ We like to feel we have a say (able to press a 'button').

◆ We are controlled by systems (can we influence the system as an individual?).

◆ Even if someone has done something, we don't always trust them.

◆ We follow and imitate others' behaviour.

◆ We follow the rules.

◆ Our power to influence is an illusion; the button is not connected to anything.

◆ The environment affects our mood and attitude.

From this 15-second story, a host of points can be made. The third step now comes into play.

The link to the outcome and message

Stories need to serve a purpose. As we have noted, stories can grab attention, create relevance, overcome resistance, establish your credibility and validate your content.

Your job is making the story *link* unambiguously clear. Because there can be several points to the same story, you need to lead the attention of participants in the meeting or presentation to the understanding that will serve your intention.

In Olivia's traffic light/silver button story, her link was empowerment.

So many employees in our business feel like a cog in some massive machine. They are functional resources, occasionally called human resources. We need to allow these complex, intelligent, experienced people to bring their best selves to work. How can we create 'silver button opportunities', where our teams are not just slaves to the system, but can have a say in how we do things around here. Not just surveys, but something they can do, every day, to demonstrate their needs and offer their opinion. We need 'silver button strategies' to involve everyone in contributing to how we work.

A simple story about crossing a busy city intersection now becomes a metaphor for allowing people to have a say in their workplace. A few months later, Olivia and her team launched the 'Silver Button Project' in her organisation. One simple story turned into a major program of work.

LINKING AS A SKILL

Some find linking easier than others. It's like a muscle; you need to work it. A good place to start is practicing similes. Something is like something is the basic structure. 'Life *is like* a box of chocolates; you never know what you are going to get', came out of Tom Hanks' mouth as the character of Forrest Gump.

We can use these at work, and people do, all the time.

- ◆ Facing the challenges of this transformation is like climbing a steep mountain. *[Link: It's tough and exhausting, but the view from the top will be worth it.]*

- ◆ Learning our new digital systems is like learning a new language. *[Link: It might be confusing at first, but it becomes easier and more fluent with practice.]*

- Creating a customised offer for you is like tailoring a suit. *[Link: It's made to fit your specific requirements and preferences.]*

- A good story is like a tattoo on the brain. *[Link: It's permanent, it's impactful and it connects to your identity.]*

Time to work

In your mind, spoken aloud or by writing it down, say, 'Life is like…' and look around you for an object. 'Life is like a keyboard.' Start coming up with statements that link to the correlation between life and a keyboard. See how many you can come up with. Practice with a colleague. This simple exercise builds linking capability, the key to effective storytelling.

Another form of linking practice is using 'As something as a something'.

- As happy as a butcher's dog.

- As cunning as a fox with a degree in cunning.

- As nervous as a small nun at a penguin shoot. (Thank you, *Blackadder*)

- As difficult as nailing jelly against a wall.

- As challenging as climbing a cliff at night without a rope.

These simple statements are evocative, require some imagination and can become memorable.

Delivering your story

Stories connect to the imagination and your emotions. The storyteller must make the story 'come alive' through voice, gesture and movement.

We were working with a very well known Sydney surgeon, hugely respected in his field, and a man of great kindness and intelligence. His storytelling was very matter of fact. This reflects his very organised, analytical mind. With encouragement and practice, he found his 'storyteller persona', and the impact on his audience and team was instantaneous. He shared with us the feedback he got from one of his team, '…we love your stories. We didn't realise you had such passion. And you could be so funny.' He is a role model for medical students and his colleagues, and his storytelling brings the reality of patients' challenges to life, including the moments where laughter also releases the tension.

Storytelling is performative. Warning: some acting is required; for example: 'Jason walked into the room looking furious. Like he had a storm cloud over his head, firing lightning bolts. Everyone stopped speaking, waiting for the torrent of anger we expected from him.'

Those are the words. You can 'become' Jason as you tell the story, looking angry and fierce, your posture carrying the energy of rage. From there you step (literally take a step) to become the nervous group expecting the wrath of Jason to descend upon them. Your posture, facial expression and energy adjusts to fearful expectation.

'I'm not an actor', is the pushback we have had many, many times. As already mentioned, work is all about performance. You act in your role. You follow the script. You make your entrances and your exits. All the world's a stage, and so on. It's not about you. It ensures the participants in the room understand your message, that they arrive at the outcome.

One morning, as I was readying for the day ahead, I had the radio on. I'm old. It's allowed. And the news story was about drug testing at music festivals in Australia. There have, tragically, been deaths at these events, as people have taken dodgy substances and paid the ultimate price. There is a call to have drug-testing labs on site so patrons can be sure the stuff they have won't kill them. The understanding here is that at music festivals, people take drugs no matter what the law might say. The objective is protecting people from harm and death. Here was my question: Why do people need to take drugs to enjoy a music festival? Why do people need to drink at parties? What is this need for chemical alteration? The answer is obvious: to reduce self-consciousness.

Let's learn to communicate in this expressive, uninhibited way without having to reach for the chardonnay, drug or whatever stimulant you care to name. This is true authenticity. Your willingness to break out of the plodding, monotone delivery of content, into an animated, expressive storyteller will be hugely welcomed by participants in your meetings and presentations.

How do we do this without taking a sneaky shot of vodka before a meeting? There is a simple, yet very effective way to develop range. It's called 'act as if'.

The concept of 'act as if' is a psychological strategy used in various contexts, including personal development, therapy and — no surprises — communication and influencing skill training.

The premise is simple yet powerful: by acting as if you already possess certain qualities or are in a certain state, you can begin to embody those qualities or that state in reality.

As we have discussed a number of times in the book, many people struggle with communication due to a lack of confidence. By *acting* as if you are confident, you will start to feel and eventually become more confident. We learnt this in Chapter 10, when we looked physiology in the PAVERS framework. Simply standing tall and walking as if you are confident will bypass your conscious brain and access your natural confidence. This is the essence of 'act as if'.

DELIVERY

By acting as if you are an experienced and engaging speaker, you can gradually improve your speaking skills. This means practicing your speech thoroughly, using confident body language, and speaking with conviction, even if you feel nervous.

Think of someone whose communication skills you admire. Act as if you *are* that person. How would they handle this meeting, conversation or presentation? This can provide a template to improve your own skills.

Remember that 'act as if' is not about overnight transformation or being inauthentic. It's about gradually adopting behaviours and mindsets that can lead to genuine growth and improvement in communication skills.

The 'act as if' technique leverages the strong connection between outward behaviours and internal states. By changing how you act, you can change how you feel and think, leading to improved skills and confidence over time. However, it's important to pair this with genuine self-reflection and skill development for lasting change.

Stories as a tool in communicating

Good stories do more than engage attention and interest, they also create a sense of connection. They build familiarity and trust and allow the listener to enter the story where they are, making them more open to learning or receptive to the ideas and content you are sharing.

Most stories can contain multiple meanings, so they are economical in conveying complex ideas in ways that are easier to grasp. We return to the vicarious experience stories provide, as close as we can to having the lived experience.

PAVERS® practice

At work, whether you are on a screen or in person, you are communicating, even if you are not saying anything. Everyone can read your energy and the quality (or lack) of your attention simply by the way you sit, stand and move.

The point is that communication is the fundamental business of being human. Of course, we communicate everywhere, and you are using the PAVERS elements all day, every day. The challenge now is to become conscious and aware of *how* you communicate along with *what* you communicate.

Conscious practice is the key of course.

In your next meeting or conversation, you could, for example, focus on auditory. 'Low and slow' could be the technique to apply. You may consciously lower your tone and speak in a more measured, managed way to ensure those around you understand you, and can sense your sincerity and depth. Low and slow — that's it.

Tomorrow, you could practice posture. Simply notice how you sit, how you stand, how you walk, consciously adjusting these physiology elements to convey authority and confidence.

Every conversation, every call, every meeting, every human-to-human situation is an opportunity to refine and develop your skills. PAVERS usage is a daily focus on constant refinement and improvement.

A final word

Mastery is a commitment to consistently improving.

In a world where rapid technological change means we don't know what jobs or professions will exist in the next 12 months or even how we will be working with game changers, such as AI, where we work and who we work with will be less defined by geography and more by contribution and value. This means how we communicate will become even more important.

This book gives you a tool for *how* to influence. It takes you through the step-by-step process of diagnosing, designing and delivering your message in every work context you will encounter.

It's now up to you to do the work of turning knowledge into behaviour.

But the learning doesn't end when you reach the last page of this book. You can access a host of resources at colinjamesmethod .com, including an AI coach to give you real-time feedback on your conciseness, clarity and how compelling you are in the way you speak and present. You can access videos on everything covered in this book. Finally, you can even practice in rehearsal rooms, where you will 'see' an audience in a large hall or around a table, with real-time feedback on your stage craft.

Contact us at info@colinjames.com.au with any comments, requests or insights you would like to share.

Thank you for being part of our community and your commitment to learning how to influence anyone, anywhere, in any context, every time.

References

Introduction

1. Colella P 2021, 'Little Italian girl talking with her hands' [video], YouTube, youtube.com/watch?v=Z5wAWyqDrnc.

2. Winerman L 2005, 'The mind's mirror', *Monitor on Psychology*, vol 36, no 9, p 48.

3. International NLP Trainers Association n.d., Marvin Oka, International NLP Trainers Association, inlpta.org/english/about/marvin-oka/#:~:text=The%20First%20Australian%20Master%20Trainer&text=Marvin%20is%20the%20Founder%20and,NLP%20Training%20Institute%20in%20Australia.

4. Cialdini R 2006, *Influence: The psychology of persuasion*, Harper Business.

5. McCarthy B 1980, *4MAT system: Teaching to learning styles with right-left mode techniques*, About Learning Inc.

Chapter 3

6. Sinek S 2011, *Start with why*, Portfolio.

7. Covey S 2020, *The 7 habits of highly effective people,* Simon & Schuster.

8. The Minto Pyramid Principle n.d., Home page, Barbaraminto.com.

Part II

9. Murch G 2016, *Fixing feedback,* Wiley.

Chapter 4

10. Cialdini R 2006, *Influence: The psychology of persuasion,* Harper Business.

11. Sinek S 2011, 'How great leaders inspire action' [video], YouTube, youtube.com/watch?v=qp0HIF3SfI4.

12. Rosling H 2011, 'Global population growth, box by box' [video], YouTube, youtube.com/watch?v=fTznEIZRkLg.

13. Brown B 2011, 'The power of vulnerability' [video], YouTube, youtube.com/watch?v=iCvmsMzlF7o.

14. Gilbert E, 2010, 'Your elusive creative genius' [video], YouTube, youtube.com/watch?v=86x-u-tz0MA.

15. Manson M 2016, *The subtle art of not giving a f*ck: A counterintuitive approach to living a good life,* Macmillan.

16. Gladwell M 2001, *The tipping point: How little things can make a big difference,* Abacus.

Chapter 9

17. Ahrendts A 2013, 'Why I believe energy can transform companies and communities', linkedin.com/pulse/20130729095958-269697626-why-i-believe-energy-can-transform-companies-and-communities/.

18. Cuddy A 2012, 'Your body language may shape who you are' [video], TED, ted.com/talks/amy_cuddy_your_body_language_may_shape_who_you_are?language=en.

Chapter 13

19. Todorov A 2017, *Face value: The irresistible influence of first impressions*, Princeton University Press.

Chapter 16

20. Fridman L 2023, #405 – Jeff Bezos: Amazon and Blue Origin [podcast], Lex Fridman Podcast, happyscribe.com/public/lex-fridman-podcast-artificial-intelligence-ai/405-jeff-bezos-amazon-and-blue-origin.

21. Chaney LD 2023, LinkedIn post, LinkedIn, linkedin.com/in/lewis-d-chaney/recent-activity/all/.

Chapter 17

22. Hinssen P 2019, 'Do you know what your company culture "smells" like?', Forbes, forbes.com/sites/peterhinssen/2019/12/17/do-you-know-what-your-company-culture-smells-like/?sh=457b07852daf.

23. LeDoux J 1998, *The emotional brain: The mysterious underpinnings of emotional life,* Simon & Schuster.

Chapter 18

24. Carnegie D 1998, *How to win friends and influence people,* Simon & Schuster.

Chapter 20

25. Campbell J 2012, *Hero with a thousand faces,* New World Library.